Army Green
Navy Blue

December 22, 1995

To Densford

Thanks for your
help in finding
this title —

Helen Joyce
Jackson

Army Green
Navy Blue

A Military Wife's Journal

By

HELEN SAYRE JACKSON

Copyright © 1995
Helen Jackson

Published by Helen Jackson
Georgetown, Texas

All Scripture: The Holy Bible,
New International Version
Copyright 1978 by New York International Bible Society

ISBN 1-57502-098-X

Additional copies may be obtained by sending a check or
money order for $10.00 U.S. (includes postage) to:

Helen Jackson
30100 Wing Foot Cove
Georgetown, TX 78628

Printed in the USA by

MORRIS
PUBLISHING
3212 E. Hwy 30
Kearney, NE 68847
800-650-7888

Dedication

To the courageous women who, most often with sacrifice, follow their men around the world: May they find comfort in Hebrews 13:5b-6: *"...Because God has said, 'Never will I leave you; never will I forsake you.' So we say with confidence, 'The Lord is my helper; I will not be afraid. What can man do to me?'"*

Acknowledgments

Jesus Christ hears my heart.

Mike Jackson, my military husband, told me to be myself.

Harold and Waneta Sayre, my parents, lovingly traveled to visit their three grandchildren.

Claire Buckingham, my first role model.

Adele McVey's no-nonsense approach to making the Army family function, gave me courage.

Debbie Ikard patiently dug with me through the stacks of my mind and depths of my heart.

Rita DeArmond believed I would hear my heart and share it with others.

Aunt Dorothy Jackson and many others prayed.

Martha Underwood, Heart for People Communications, Georgetown, Texas, provided technical support.

Connie G. Giles of Austin, Texas, edited; another friend helped in the initial stages.

Francis W. Heatherley, Balcony Author Services, Austin, Texas, promised to help get my words published, and he was faithful to do it.

Table of Contents

Chapter 1

In the Army Now

"For I know the plans I have for you," declares the Lord, "plans to prosper you and not to harm you, plans to give you hope and a future. Then you will call upon me and come and pray to me, and I will listen to you. You will seek me and find me when you seek me with all your heart." Jeremiah 29:11-13

In 1967, my husband, Mike, discontent building homes with his father, Lyman, and convinced he was called to the military, applied for active duty after serving six years with the Marine Corps Reserves and the National Guard. He assured me if Army life ever became too difficult for me or our two small daughters, Kathy and Kristy, he'd get out.

Initially, I was torn between complying with his decision and fulfilling my dream of rearing the girls near my parents' farm. I'd lived in the same farmhouse my first eighteen years, and what little time my family had spent traveling by car had seemed boring and a waste of time.

Having had few big challenges and with little sense of adventure, I saw no need to uproot our young family. Nearly every one of my friends, whose husbands farmed or worked in factories, asked, "You're leaving the security of a family business to do *what*?" Bowing to the inevitable, though, I wished I'd been more attentive to the stories of military life in the Marine Corps told by Lyman and by Mike's older brother, Ron.

Preparing to move from central Indiana, I told people in our little farming community I welcomed the prospect of traveling. I meant I intended to fly back often and to overlook no excuse to take Mike up on his promise to leave active duty if I couldn't adjust. I testified at church that the Lord sold our house the same day Mike received a telegram welcoming him to active duty. Privately, I grumbled to the One who did it. I didn't mean to mislead anyone, but I was totally aware that I was unprepared for pulling up stakes and becoming a nomad.

Humble yourselves, therefore, under God's mighty hand, that he may lift you up in due time. Cast all your anxiety on him because he cares for you.
I Peter 5:6-7

Written orders arrived. We were going to Fort Hood, Texas. My friends asked, "Where is that?" I soon learned that a military family does nothing, even going on vacation, without written instructions based solely on the Army's needs.

Despite Mike's enthusiasm to embark on this adventure, I didn't like having strangers contracted by the government swarming into my home at 7:30 a.m., snatching possessions and shoving them into packing boxes. Neither did I enjoy the prospect of traveling more than 1,000 miles south and west in the summer with my little girls. Kathy was 2 1/2, and Kristy was only ten months old. I suspected the further we drove in our little station wagon, the more miserably hot we'd become.

I complained to my friend Linda Jones, and she offered to ride with the girls and me to Texas if her folks were willing to watch her children and if Mike would buy her a one-way ticket back to Indiana. I'd taken only one airplane trip, and as much as I cared about Linda, I was fairly certain I would not make her the same offer.

Linda explained that she saw my trip as an adventure, and she wanted to be a part of it. Her parents agreed to stay with her kids, and Mike jumped at the ticket deal. I was convinced that since he and I wouldn't be traveling in tandem, he thought the chances of my finding Fort Hood were better with Linda along than if I started out by myself. She could help with the children and assure me that we were having a great trip.

I looked into the tiny rearview mirror as my station wagon chugged away from the back door of my parents' farmhouse, but I could see nothing but tears. I had no idea whether the clothing, toys, or baby gear we'd packed in the back would be what I needed once I got to Texas. Outside of making one wrong turn and sleeping in one dumpy motel, Linda and I had no difficulty playing the role of modern-day pioneers.

Trust in him at all times, O people; pour out your hearts to him, for God is our refuge. Psalm 62:8

A military post is fenced so that everyone knows its boundaries. Inside the fence, space is allocated for activities associated with everyday living, and the rest is devoted to serious military training.

Families reside in quarters (apartments or houses, not coins). Upon reporting for duty, a military man with a family puts his name on the waiting list for quarters and then goes off post to find a temporary home.

Mike found a place the first morning of his search, even though rentals were scarce. When the girls and I arrived a week or so after Mike, military neighbors quickly surrounded me with helping hands. The women shared their hopes, dreams, remedies for heat rash, and lists of baby sitters. They advised me to get some engraved calling cards and told me what to wear when I went with Mike for social calls. Each one had her own reason for affirming my need for a military photo I.D.

Getting that card wasn't a matter of choice, but necessity. It would verify I was Mike's dependent. I didn't care for the term *dependent*; I thought it implied I was an encumbrance, not a blessing, to my husband. But the card would allow me access to the commissary (grocery store) and the exchange (department store). I'd have to have the card to obtain medical care for the girls and me. The fact that services and goods provided on post were generally less costly than those outside the fence was an enticement, as well.

Those who'd been there longer than a month said I'd be wise to budget carefully, or I'd find myself in a commissary check-out line on payday with the hundreds, perhaps thousands, of others whose pantries were bare. *Every* facility was as crowded as the area's housing. Everywhere I went, I was forced to stand in line, and the process of procuring an I.D. was no exception. Even though the girls waited in line with me, they wouldn't need *cards* until they were ten years old.

Finally, equipped with my own card and bombarded with information and encouragement from the other wives, I began to suspect that if our household goods weren't delayed or lost in transit, I might be able to make our rented, temporary house cozy. I might even find enthusiasm to adjust to our new life.

Without my *stuff*, I was forced to concentrate on the negative aspects of my surroundings. My back hurt from sleeping on the floor. The girls were bored without the bulk of their toys. Stifling heat penetrated not only the windows and doors, but also the brick walls. The one window air-conditioner we purchased in haste struggled to cool the living room, which absorbed the afternoon sun.

Our government workers might not know why our things had been delayed, but on the brighter side, I was convinced I knew Someone who did. I prayed in desperation, asking Him to deliver my things.

My prayer was answered the very next morning. About 10:30, with outside temperatures already soaring into the high eighties, a moving van stopped in front of my house. The driver, who introduced himself as Joe Myers, explained that the initial driver had become ill and abandoned the truck.

"Soon's I got the word, I came nonstop, fast as I could," he said. "I don't really know why, but I just felt like I should."

I knew why, and I sent a silent thank-you to the One responsible.

I welcomed the arrival of the van with great relief and enthusiasm. Now we could get rid of the Army's green field table which graced the kitchen and the mattresses that served as beds and sofa and begin to settle in! Kathy was even more excited than I was.

"I need my pegboard and my tricycle," she informed Mr. Myers in no uncertain terms.

"Coming right up," he answered with a grin. Of course, he and I knew moving vans have to be unloaded as items become accessible.

But Kathy was too young to understand. She waited impatiently near the huge truck for her things to appear. As she waited, her thick, dark hair began to look as if it had been plastered to her moist head.

"Come on in, honey," I urged. "It's too hot out there."

"I need my tricycle," she repeated. Hands on her hips, she kept asking for her toys each time Mr. Myers or his helper came out of the truck.

Finally, she received her toys, all in good shape. A smile lit up her face as she thanked the men. Her little body quivered with excitement as I quickly tightened the bolts loosened in the trip. She began playing immediately.

Kathy's possessions had come through unscathed, but mine were a little more dented, marred, scratched, and rubbed than when they'd gone into the van in Indiana. The men who'd packed and loaded our things had carefully attached a little sticky number on each piece of furniture and box before loading it, leaving me with five thin sheets of paper describing my stuff and its condition. It was my job on the receiving end to check off each number on *my* copy of the paper inventory and inspect for damages as the movers carried our possessions into the house and garage. Mike came home as the movers finished and signed all the papers associated with the move, indicating that all of our things had finally been delivered.

Once we'd put our possessions in order, Mike and I were amused at what we'd learned about moving from a land of changing seasons to another where one perpetually mows the lawn. We'd sold our lawn mower and given away our hoses and sprinklers, deciding they were dirty and might damage other things in transit. But we'd brought the snow shovel to Texas because it was new and clean!

Do you not know? Have you not heard? The Lord is the everlasting God, the Creator of the ends of the earth. He will not grow tired or weary, and his understanding no one can fathom. Isaiah 40:28

Even though the other young women were very helpful in sharing what would be expected of me, Mike told me to be myself. I did my best to embrace military custom and protocol. Basically, that meant respecting the way military communities had functioned in the past and graciously carrying on those traditions.

But finding the balance between my expectations and everyone else's, I found, was tiring. Isolated from everything which to me represented security, I didn't know for sure who I was. I felt like the proverbial square peg--a mother of two in a sea of newly-weds. In adjusting to my new life, I had to be even more organized than other "transplanted and bewildered" folks without children. Lining up a baby sitter for an upcoming two-hour social event could turn into a twelve-hour chore if the post hosted another activity more alluring than getting paid to watch the Jacksons' children.

My well-behaved daughters trooped right along with the other ladies and me to military parades. Attending one with them gave me the same sense of patriotism I'd experienced in Mrs. Swartz's first- and second-grade classes while reciting the Pledge of Allegiance. As I put my right hand over my heart to pay respect to my nation's flag, I felt myself an integral part of a wonderful nation. Enduring heat, the smell of diesel fuel, the noise of rumbling tanks, and sand-blasted teeth invigorated me. The sights, sounds, and smells of soldiers and tanks passing the reviewing stands made me forget I'd dressed as if I were going to church, complete with hat and gloves, and that I'd had to show my I.D. card to pass the gate guards.

But an occasional parade didn't take away the daily loneliness of being over 1,000 miles from the farm. I felt as if I were being asked to juggle God, family, and duty to country while standing under a heat lamp, balanced on one leg.

Surrounded by the big State of Texas, I learned anyone not in the military is a civilian. In the strictest sense, the girls and I were civilians. But we were a *military* family living in a town where folks weren't eager, it seemed, to welcome those who'd be staying only temporarily. Perhaps they sensed I didn't want to be in their town. Civilian neighbors only nodded their heads in our direction when the girls and I took our early morning or late evening walks. They never initiated any conversation. The town's merchants eyed us warily, and a few church members asked if our young family was *military* in a tone of voice that sounded more like a statement than a question.

An eight-year-old girl named Mindy, who lived on our
street, ventured into our yard one day while the girls and I
played in their wading pool. She flitted in, wearing her pink-
and-white polka-dotted bathing suit, briefly splashed some
water on herself, and then turned her attention to me. She
wanted to talk; I was willing to listen. In return for my
listening ear, she gave me an inkling of why I was being
ignored.

"You know we call this place the ghost house, don't you?"

"No, I don't. Can you tell me why?"

"Well, no one ever stays here long. We get tired of meeting
new people and then Poof!" she threw both hands and arms
into the air above her head, "they're gone!"

As if reciting a prepared monologue, she told me it upset
her to have military kids move in and out and in and out of her
neighborhood. As she used the words "in and out," she turned
her oval face first toward her right shoulder and then to the
left, causing her long, blonde curls to bounce on the opposite
thin shoulder. She said it hurt her to make a new friend and
then have to tell her good-bye. One who'd lived in this house
before us had promised to write her letters, but she never did.
Mindy had observed children sad to leave her yet at the same
time eagerly anticipating their next homes. She thought about
them sometimes.

Suddenly she grew very quiet, her animation stopped. Then
she looked at me as if she and I were the only two people on
earth. After a few seconds of silence, she said, very matter-of-
factly, "I hate war."

She didn't wait for me to agree or defend our living on her
street; I'd heard her heart. She didn't have to tell me that it's
easier never to say hello than to suffer through another
farewell. She left to visit her civilian friends, and the girls and I
never saw her again.

Perhaps being accepted by the civilian population wasn't
top priority. But I was even more sobered to learn that not

only were Mike's active duty exercises more concentrated than his reserve training had been, but also the sole purpose of the training was to prepare soldiers for war as quickly as possible. The intensive training schedule combined with the unit's not having as many men as needed made Mike's workday long. While the girls napped, I wrote letters to my parents. I wish they'd said, "Dear Mother and Daddy, All is well here in frontier land, and we are contented." Instead, they revealed the heart of a lonely young woman. Sometimes I cried as I put my tales of woe into the mailbox.

Occasionally, on a Sunday afternoon when the rates were least expensive, I went to the wall-mounted kitchen telephone and dialed "O." A few times, the long-distance operator answered quickly and systematically pushed my call through to Mother's telephone far away. More often I summoned the operator's attention for fifteen to thirty minutes before she gave me her undivided attention. Mother and I compared weather (mine was always hotter), and I listened as she related details of recent weddings and births of our friends and neighbors. It wouldn't have mattered to me what Mother talked about; I merely needed to hear her voice to give me the courage to ease into another week.

Twice a week, I wrestled fatigues (sturdy green work uniforms), starched stiffly enough to stand alone. Because no air could get through the clogged pores of this clothing, the salt of a soldier's perspiration melted with the starch and formed big white blotches on the outside of his shirt. Often he'd change uniforms more than once a day. A wife either laundered and starched the monstrosities at home or delivered them to the commercial laundry. For me, the trip in my non-air-conditioned car with two tikes in tow was anything but pleasant. Nevertheless, the trip was better than the prospect of laundering the fatigues at home.

At the laundry, my daughters were usually given lollipops, which they wanted me to unwrap immediately. By the time I managed to trade several sets of the smelly uniforms for cleaner, stiffer ones, unwrap the lollipops given to my sweet children, and travel back home with rigid clothing and squirming, sticky bodies, I'd had it. *I* was fatigued.

Taking the girls to the post nursery while I made such jaunts was out of the question. It was one thing to have strangers in charge of possessions, but quite another to relinquish sobbing offspring to them. My mother's heart couldn't and wouldn't subject itself to that kind of tearing-away unless absolutely necessary.

A newly arrived military wife and mother learned not only a totally new routine, but also a new vocabulary. When Mike had been in the Marine Reserves, what I'd called a uniform jacket he'd called a *blouse*. Now, on active duty with the Army, even *he* sometimes got confused and called the Army's latrine by the Marine term *head*. Whatever the individual military services chose to call it, I continued to instruct the girls to use the word *potty*. Mike was lucky to get to come home for meals, I thought. The single men from the barracks ate in the *mess hall*. Nothing sounded less appetizing.

A wife also needed to learn how to relate to others in the military, whether they worked with her husband or not. That added responsibility meant learning about rank. Mother had always called bacon rank when it had been in the refrigerator too long and needed to be tossed. But "rank" in the Army had nothing to do with a wife's fatigue or anything smelling bad. Rank indicated the pay grade and duties assigned, based on the longevity and expertise of military personnel. Mike instructed me to respect the hard work and acceptance of responsibility of each rank. To help me recognize the insignia that indicated rank, he bought a book with charts and photos for me to study when I had free time.

I studied. Nevertheless, when confronted by masses of green-clad personnel, I had difficulty remembering what the little rank patches sewn onto the fatigues of each wearer meant. Because I didn't see well from a distance, I seldom could read the name tag. So, to keep from insulting anyone or embarrassing my husband, I called everyone in his unit "sir," just to be safe. I certainly didn't want my slow adaptation to reflect poorly on Mike's reputation.

As I looked around the post, I found myself fascinated by the huge metal trailers on a lot near the Commissary Annex. It was reported they contained large machines which kept volumes of information on a reel-to-reel tape. Someday, it was rumored, those *new-fangled* machines (computers, I think they called them) would "talk" to similar machines in Washington, D.C., eliminating the need for so much paperwork!

Chapter 2

Tour Of Duty

. . . if on some point you think differently, that too God will make clear to you. Philippians 3:15b

As I watched wives send their husbands away for the one-year combat assignment to the Republic of Vietnam early in 1968, I realized I was not alone in my confusion and misery. Some wives lashed out at their husbands and the Army. Others welcomed the opportunity to pick up the reins as head of the household. I decided that when Mike left for Vietnam, if given the option, the girls and I would return to Indiana while Mike was away. We wouldn't stay at Fort Hood, where faces changed daily because folks were *ordered* into and out of the area.

I have realized since that I was selfish. By focusing on my needs, I neglected others who could have benefited from a comforting word. My heart ached for the family of the First Sergeant whose son drowned, but I did nothing. Others hurt from the effects of infidelity, alcohol, or money mismanagement; I avoided their company. I was repulsed by an older wife's announcement that combat pay would buy furniture a military family otherwise couldn't afford.

Time passed. When the girls and I succumbed to strep throat simultaneously, Mike bought our first color TV, hoping his ailing family would be entertained while he worked practically around the clock. I was still not happy with Army life.

My son, pay attention to what I say; listen closely to my words. Do not let them out of your sight, keep them within your heart. Proverbs 4:20-21

Just when I was tempted to decide I was too miserable and lonely to stay in central Texas, old Colonel Armstrong (he must have been old; he had white hair) gave me an added dimension to consider. He pulled me aside after a parade and talked to me as if I were his daughter.

"Helen," he said, "it appears to me that you are miserable and need to learn a lot more about being flexible."

My mind raced. I wondered what I'd *done* to be singled out for this critique.

Perhaps twice my age, the weathered gentleman didn't elaborate. Yet his intuitive words burned their way through my emotions and forced stinging tears into my eyes. The concerned look in his peaceful green eyes and his gentle handshake let me know he meant no harm.

I was courteous in respect to his age and rank, but as I watched him go, I saw no need for immediate change. As far as I was concerned, I *was* flexible. I had come to Texas and learned of scorpions and snakes when I would have preferred to stay in Indiana and watch the changing seasons.

While driving home, though, I began to question if the source of my misery could be the result of my own lack of flexibility. I wondered if what I saw as being organized, the seasoned colonel saw as regimentation. Had he given his advice because he'd discerned that my attitude wasn't contributing positively to Mike's morale?

I did not have long to ponder this issue before another wave of change hit our household. Because most of Mike's peers had no children, Mike's name worked its way quickly to the top of the waiting list for post housing. We moved into a lovely set of three-bedroom, centrally air-conditioned

quarters. Its indoor laundry area and washable walls were the
first features my heart embraced. The fact that water, sewage,
garbage collection, maintenance, and electricity were part of
the "rent" made a more lasting impression. But physical
comforts and more pennies in my pockets didn't help me find
the balance between accepting a supporting role in America's
defense and clinging to my postponed dreams.

Every other week another moving van pulled onto our
street, gobbled up another family's stuff, and rolled away.

*Therefore be clear minded and self-controlled so
that you can pray.* I Peter 4:7b

During the first twelve months of Mike's active duty, the
girls and I returned to Indiana three times. I kept one foot in
what had once been childhood security, but was now civilian,
while I cautiously explored my national defense environment
with the other.

Abruptly, Mike received the Permanent Change of Station
orders I'd dreaded, but I took consolation in the fact that the
same document which ordered Mike to Vietnam also
authorized transporting the girls and me, with our belongings,
back to Indiana.

Within three weeks of the orders arriving, I finished
teaching Vacation Bible School, sold Mike's little car, made
arrangements with the government to move our things,
notified Mike's parents I'd like them to find the girls and me
an apartment in Indiana, and watched as a loaded moving van
once again pulled away from my front door. We'd been in the
Fort Hood area thirteen months and ten days.

It was the 50-pound knots in my stomach that were
difficult to ignore. When I asked a doctor at the hospital for
something to help untie the knots, he chided, "There are some

things medications won't help. You must make up your mind to cope and then do it."

I gulped, checked the girls' and my medical records out of the hospital, and headed back to our quarters to clean as if my life depended upon passing the rigid *clearing quarters* inspection.

Clearing quarters had both its good and bad aspects. I worked diligently to clean away every crumb and dust speck, wash windows and walls, and fill nail holes with toothpaste. It was exhilarating to stand there with the inspector and hear, "You passed." On the other hand, my sense of accomplishment was counter-balanced by thoughts that I didn't have a place to call home and strangers once again were in charge of my *stuff*.

Mike had the look of a man with a mission as he left briefly for TDY (temporary duty) to Panama's jungles in preparation for going to war in a similar climate. Somewhat apprehensive, I worked amidst moving boxes in Indiana while he was gone. Late nights I tried not to think about his leaving the girls and me for a *long* period of time or what might be required of him once he reached his combat unit.

While I dreaded being separated from him for the year's tour, Mike was eager to get to Southeast Asia. He wanted to put his military training to the test. He'd also promised his mother, Margaret, that when he arrived there, her youngest son, Tony, would be given an early release from his 'Nam unit and sent back to the U.S.

Calling a combat assignment a tour seemed senseless. I knew nothing about war, but instinctively knew that Mike's assignment in a war zone wouldn't be fun. A mere year and a half earlier, I'd known little about Vietnam and its history, despite the fact that my brother-in-law, Ron, had gone there with a map-making team. Now, because of U.S. involvement and my husband's temporary occupation as a warrior, I not

only learned some world history, but also faced an uncertain
future.

*I tell you the truth, anyone who gives you a cup of
water in my name because you belong to Christ will
certainly not lose his reward.* Mark 9:41

Looking into the mirror, I searched for the bright and
confident farm girl who'd married her high school sweetheart
and later told him she would become an Army wife, if leaving
the farmlands would make him happy.

I remember Mike's departure with perfect clarity. Bravely,
I watched him say good-bye to our grandmothers, parents,
and daughters. Although I had to believe Mike would return
safely, I wanted to tell him good-bye privately. Mother cared
for the girls while I escorted Mike to Indianapolis to catch his
flight. Despite my desire to be bravely independent and in
control of my emotions, once Mike's plane left the gate, the
huge knots in my stomach reached up and grabbed my throat.
I froze, incapable of thinking or acting coherently.

God, not surprised by what He saw, placed a woman to my
immediate left who had come to send her husband off on a
business trip. Seeing my distress, she gently put her arm
around my shoulder and led me to the airport coffee shop
where she bought us coffee and listened as I tearfully poured
out my anxieties.

Neither of us talked about our faith, but in her response to
my need, I saw the God of all Creation had not left nor
forsaken me. I have no knowledge of her reward, but I shall
never forget her kindness.

Be strong and take heart, all you who hope in the Lord. Psalm 31:24

Mike and I decided I wouldn't join him for R & R (rest and recreation) in Hawaii as others who'd gone recommended. Even with the added monthly combat pay and the government's bearing the cost of Mike's flight from Vietnam to Hawaii, we were convinced we couldn't afford the luxury of my air fare, five days in a hotel, and eating in restaurants. Nevertheless, after Mike had been in country ten days and shuffled from one unit to another, he sent a letter stating he wanted all three of his girls to meet him in Hawaii.

Mike's parents decided to come along. Not every wife shared R & R with her children and in-laws. But all of us enjoyed the few days of Mike's respite from the war. He'd been wounded the month before our rendezvous, and each adult needed to see with his or her own eyes that Mike would recover. All too soon, the brief vacation was over.

As we saw Mike off, I looked down at Kathy, barely four years old now, crumpled and clutching her baby doll she'd received for Christmas seven weeks earlier. I marveled at her courage. Before we'd left our Waikiki hotel, I'd cautioned her not to cry until her daddy was inside the airplane that would take him back to "work."

Lyman and Margaret bid Mike "aloha" inside the terminal and watched as their little granddaughters and I walked as far as we were allowed. Despite his devotion to his country and its Army, Mike's hesitancy to leave us showed as he headed for the big bird. I diverted my eyes from the mechanical vulture poised to snatch my lover, my friend from me.

I don't remember there being one tear shed until the girls and I turned to rejoin Mike's parents. At that second, Kathy collapsed and began to sob uncontrollably. When she pulled the plug on her ocean of tears, I realized the extent of her fortitude and pain. She had obediently honored my request not to give in to emotion in Mike's presence, thus preventing her tears from wounding her daddy where no bandage could reach.

As I could not coax her to move toward the terminal, her grandfather came outside, and in his strong arms he gathered the broken heart encased in Kathy's small body.

When Kathy's tears had dried, we headed for the mainland. I felt as if every ounce of my energy had been drained, and I wondered how I would find the strength to face six more months without Mike.

On leave, Mike and I had spent money we thought we wouldn't have, buying a taste of paradise and a smidgeon of courage.

> . . . I have set before you life and death, blessings and curses. Now choose life, so that you and your children may live and that you may love the Lord your God, listen to his voice, and hold fast to him.
> Deuteronomy 30:19b-20a

Being slightly visually impaired, I've not always seen with my eyes what others saw (perhaps part of the reason I disliked traveling by automobile). However, having given my heart to Jesus when I was less than six years old assured me that He had directed and would direct my paths. What others observed as coincidence, I often saw as a direct result of my telling Jesus that I needed His help. My parents led me into the understanding that I could take every concern directly to God. I trusted my parents; therefore, I found it easy to trust *our* heavenly Father.

So why was I having so much difficulty, at this point in my life, telling God my concerns and trusting Him to intervene?

Why did I now want to *see* the answer before I could have faith that He, not circumstances, was stretching me? Why did I suspect He might not continue the work He'd begun in me as a child? Were my adult problems really that much bigger and more complicated than those of my childhood? Or was it that I had listened to the misguided teaching that "God helps those who help themselves," hampering what He'd planned for me? It was evident that the more energy and focus I put into my problems, the bigger they seemed to become.

While in Hawaii, I had attempted to look beyond Mike's bandages and envision our future. Fully convinced I had made concessions many 25-year-olds would never be asked to make, I yearned for our contribution to national security to end. Mike, on the other hand, wanted to pursue formal education when he returned Stateside, thereby enabling him to remain on active duty.

At home, I realized Kathy's obedience at the airport had drawn my thoughts back to my being obedient as a child. Even though I could not *see* the Lord's hand in my current situation, I acknowledged that if I wanted to stay happily married to the man I loved, I would need to lay down my selfish desires and become flexibly involved (with God's help) in Mike's world, for he needed to march to the drum beating within him.

God, I sensed, was calling me back to my child-like faith and trust in Him. He wanted our relationship to grow. He wanted me to grow up. He'd desired to help me from the beginning, not just when I'd done all I could do and was at my wit's end.

He who fears the Lord has a secure fortress, and for his children it will be a refuge. The fear of the Lord is a fountain of life, turning a man from the snares of death. Proverbs 14:26-27

The responsibilities associated with rearing the girls by myself remained my biggest concern. I'd particularly depended upon Mike's wisdom and intuition when an episode of minor illness hit. He instinctively knew whether to take a feverish child to the doctor or not, but the Power of Attorney he'd left with me to handle our business affairs didn't help much when one of the girls didn't feel well. I needed the balance of Mike's firm voice and the tenderness of my heart to know when to tell a daughter to "dry up" the tears as Mike would have done and when to let her sit in my lap for a prolonged session of comforting.

At Fort Hood my own need for personal security and stability had, more often than not, overshadowed my devotion to our Stars and Stripes. Yet, here in my old stomping grounds, where I'd once felt as if my life was complete, my self-confidence now seemed tied to letters Mike wrote daily, but which arrived in my mailbox in batches.

Spending time as a lone parent and handling family finances, all the while yearning and praying for my husband's safe return, did, however, bring some measure of maturity. The Faithful One who'd answered my childhood prayers knew my insecurities, delivered me from fear of darkness, and helped me carry out responsibilities I'd once considered Mike's. The girls and I lived only five miles from the farmhouse where I'd grown up, and we knew we were always welcome there. Mother encouraged me and prayed for Mike diligently, while Daddy entertained the girls with games and stories. He assured me, as apprehensive as I was with Mike's being away, that my suppressed joy would surface once again.

I am the Lord your God, who teaches you what is best for you, who directs you in the way you should go. If only you had paid attention to my commands,

your peace would have been like a river, your righteousness like the waves of the sea.
Isaiah 48:17b-18

Tom and Judy Leach, a couple with whom we went to church, and their two young daughters, Kim and Amy, often invited us to share an evening in their home or at the park-- doing things as a family with a daddy Mike's age.

Most other civilians with whom I associated didn't know what to say and stayed away. They weren't openly opposed to the war so much as they seemed busy and uncomfortable hearing about my love/hate relationship with the nightly news (a daily update of the war's casualties). Just as I hadn't known how to help hurting ones while I was in Texas, the majority of my friends, some of whom I'd known for years, didn't know how to encourage me.

Create in me a pure heart, O God, and renew a steadfast spirit within me. Do not cast me from your presence or take your Holy Spirit from me. Restore to me the joy of your salvation and grant me a willing spirit, to sustain me. Psalm 51:10-12

Ironically, while I sat in the confines of my Indiana apartment questioning where we were headed, God used a letter from a military officer's wife to give me insight. I'd not talked to Claire Buckingham much at Fort Hood, even though I saw her at church each Sunday. She'd never admonished me as Colonel Armstrong had done--what I'd learned from her was mostly by observation.

She dressed conservatively. Her children, older than mine, were interesting conversationalists, allowed to be kid-like after church, but expected to behave as a young lady and gentlemen should. It was obvious she had trained them at home so they knew without her having to say a word what was expected of them in public. It was rumored she entertained creatively; her reputation as a woman of faith was known to all.

When her letter arrived, I was astounded. In the midst of her moving and serving, and during a period of national upheaval, she remembered *me*! She included her new address, snatches of family news, and a reminder of her gratitude that we (she and I) were privileged to serve as Christian military wives.

It was a beautiful letter sent to many, no doubt, but there was a lesson to be learned from her selflessness. She juggled family, community, and church responsibilities, yet remained mindful of a lonely, isolated young woman far away. In sending me that letter, she'd *chosen* to consider me her friend. Perhaps if I were to emulate her, I would find practical answers.

> *Seek the Lord while he may be found; call on him while he is near. Let the wicked forsake his way and the evil man his thoughts. Let him turn to the Lord, and he will have mercy on him, and to our God, for he will freely pardon.* Isaiah 55:6-7

With each day's passing and Mike still away, I became more comfortable with the knowledge the U.S. Army would eventually take us, once again, outside Indiana's borders. When my long, lonely days dragged into nights, my friend Jesus talked to me through His Word, written centuries earlier. I found it difficult to comprehend how He knew so far in advance what I'd need to comfort my heart on any given day. Many times, as I looked among the pages of my Bible, a sentence or two seemed to jump off the pages and penetrate my heart, giving me the assurance that He knew my thoughts and emotions. Interestingly enough, by reading what He said about who I was in Him, I began to understand that, thus far, I'd merely taken baby steps toward comprehending the maturity He wanted me to achieve.

> *Still another said, "I will follow you, Lord; but first let me go back and say good-by to my family." Jesus replied, "No one who puts his hand to the plow and looks back is fit for service in the kingdom of God."*
> Luke 9:61-62

Might it be that, just as God called each of His children to do His work on earth, He called interesting women of varying ages from different areas of the country to add stability to constantly changing military communities? Was there someone else out there besides Jesus and Mrs. B who understood those things formulated in my heart but not quite solidified enough to bring out into the open?

Was there a possibility I really was better equipped to leave family and friends than I'd been two years earlier?

Gathering up all the courage I could find, I was fairly confident that once my little family moved to a new post, I'd be able to find my niche. Though I might not appear to be more flexible, I knew my heart beat with a little more purpose than before my trip to Honolulu. I wouldn't try to convince anyone else in my tiny farm town of the changes going on in my heart, but I vowed to remember some of the initial struggles of military life so those following would know I'd once heard their hearts.

But you will not leave in haste or go in flight; for the Lord will go before you, the God of Israel will be your rear guard. Isaiah 52:12

Checking off the days on my calendar one at a time, I hoped we'd move to a post other than Fort Hood. Not only were the summers there too hot, I didn't care to be reminded of my wobbly beginnings in the Army community. But I'd made the decision to commit to the military way of life, no matter where, and now I wanted to get started.

Waiting for Mike to finish his tour grated on my nerves. The closer I came to planning his homecoming, the more difficult it was to keep my hands and mind constructively busy. During waking hours, my mind tried unsuccessfully to mesh the hopes for world peace with the facts I'd gathered from Mike's letters and the national news broadcasts. At night when sleep would not come, I pictured in my mind how I'd fix my hair and what I'd wear to the airport to meet Mike. With each day's passing, I knew my chances of getting Mike back were better than the month, the week, or even the day before.

Whether I wanted to admit it or not, every prayer for Mike's safe return grew out of the realization that there was the possibility of its not happening. Only once during that time had I been traumatized by a government car driving by my apartment. I'd heard if Mike were killed, there would be two men, one of them a chaplain, come to my door to break the news. Even though I saw that the men in the government car weren't looking for our house, my heart raced for a second, and then nearly stopped.

For me to find *my* niche, Mike would have to come home. Of course, I knew roughly when his tour would end, but I needed details! He had purposely not written down or even tried to remember my unlisted telephone number so that if he fell into the hands of the enemy, the girls and I wouldn't be contacted by anyone who didn't need to talk to us. Therefore, I didn't expect him to call me with his flight information, but I searched his letters to find the date and time of his arrival back in the World, as the troops called the U.S. Each day while I worked on the girls' and my dresses that we'd wear to the airport reunion, I watched for Mr. Kimmerling, our mail carrier, to approach our rural mailbox in his blue pick-up, take the letter I'd written to Mike, and hopefully bring me at least one in return.

Was there a letter? If so, did it contain flight information? Each day I searched and was disappointed. The information I sought just didn't come.

Then at 5:30 a.m. on a Thursday morning in 1969, a week before I expected Mike to come home, the telephone rang. I immediately sensed it wasn't bad news, as usually comes at that hour of the morning. But I never dreamed Mike was calling from San Francisco!

Even though I usually become coherent when my head lifts from the pillow, when I heard Mike say, "Good morning," I blurted out, "Where are you?"

"I'm in San Francisco. Is that okay with you?"

He explained that he had suddenly become a part of President Nixon's initial pullout, leaving Vietnam a week early. He was waiting for a flight to Indianapolis and would be home before noon.

I began to ramble on that the house wasn't clean, the dresses weren't finished, and I needed a haircut. Mike understood I wanted everything perfect for his homecoming and that I had to rerun my preparation list through my head before I could assess that his coming early was better than my being perfectly prepared. He chuckled, and then said, "Oh, by the way, you don't have to call Mom and Dad. I had to call them to get your phone number."

It was too early to call anyone else with my good news, but I called Lyman and Margaret to ask what time they thought

we should leave for Indy. I didn't wake the girls; they needed
to sleep as long as possible so *their* wait would be minimal.

I quickly dusted the furniture, tossing away the letter I'd
planned to mail to Mike, and mopped the kitchen floor.

Then, as I hopped into the shower, trying to decide what to
wear, I began to cry. The tears of relief landed at my feet and
disappeared down the drain, leaving me with the sense that
uncertainty, for this day anyway, had passed.

Chapter 3

One In Spirit

But Ruth replied, "Don't urge me to leave you or to turn back from you. Where you go I will go, and where you stay I will stay. Your people will be my people and your God my God." Ruth 1:16

Mike returned, but the warmth of his homecoming was tempered by the stark realization that he brought home a year's experiences about which I knew nothing. He carefully protected me from those memories, which now served to separate his professional life from our private one.

Hearing his soft, steady snoring beside me camouflaged the enormous commitment I'd made to rear our daughters wherever Uncle Sam sent us. I'd pictured in my mind our being inseparable when reunited, only to discover Mike's military and civilian classes at our new post, Fort Knox, Kentucky, (home of Armor and the nation's gold vault), kept him away from me six days and most evenings each week.

Furthermore, Mike bought a sports car, took up golf, and once went deer hunting with the guys. I had to accept that during this period of adjustment, he was more comfortable sharing experiences with those men who knew his heart than with me. Although not rejected, I sensed a thin, invisible partition kept us from truly being one.

Restoring Mike's and Kristy's relationship took time, too. When he'd left, she'd been a toddler and "Daddy's girl." But she snubbed him for weeks after his return. When he offered to help her with a task, her blue eyes looked squarely into his, and she announced, "My mommy will help me, thank you."

I did not quit dreaming, but I began relinquishing my dreams to the One who knew better than I what my little family needed. At Fort Hood I had merely attempted to play the role of a military wife. Now, with my mind and heart involved, I invested commitment, trusting I'd reap flexibility. Every other woman at Knox seemed to understand my roller-coaster emotions without my having to say a word. Her husband, too, was either returning from or preparing to go to Southeast Asia or West Germany.

At Fort Hood most of the Army wives seemed to have met their husbands in high school or college, or been introduced by a relative or mutual friend. But here in a school setting, I began to see and appreciate the extent God worked to put some married couples together. I was most attracted to a woman reared on a farm in Kansas who'd married a fellow from New York City and one from Okinawa whose husband had grown up in North Carolina.

Amidst my true transition from civilian to military living, Kathy entered kindergarten, and Mike encouraged me to "live a little." While many others expected or tended post-war babies, I headed to the hospital, with my increased maturity and resolve, to work as a volunteer. I envisioned myself becoming like the woman at the Indianapolis airport--one with compassion and encouragement for others and the wisdom to know what to say and when to remain silent. Someday I wanted to be like Mrs. B, known as a woman of faith.

During this time of settling, still encumbered with a bit of emotional baggage from being separated, Mike and I tried to make financial plans and set long-term goals. However, *long-term* translated into a year and a half. It had been predicted Mike would have an 18-month "turn-around time" between Vietnam assignments. With that possibility in mind, Lyman built a duplex for us in Indiana, anticipating that Mike would again be assigned to a place he couldn't take his dependents.

. . .Jonathan became one in spirit with David. . .
I Samuel 18:1b

Just before Mike completed his military schooling at Fort Knox, he was ordered to stay at the Armor School as "permanent party." We elected, then, to move from up-and-down students' quarters to a one-story duplex on Corley Street, a few blocks away.

I watched as Linda Seward hesitantly walked up my front steps and then turned back toward her quarters. Somehow I knew she had crossed Corley Street and walked up the hill to welcome me to her neighborhood. She looked as if she were physically tired, yet there was a spring in her step.

Later in the day, when she'd gathered more courage, she and I bonded instantly.

Barely adults ourselves, we were attempting to nurture five small children. In a matter of days, each of us was able to anticipate and respond when the other needed an extra pair of hands. We shared recipes, hobbies, and stories of our differing childhoods. We compared the changes an unpopular war brought into our lives.

Linda and I loved to laugh, and we faced Corley Street's highs and lows with humor. While other neighbors thought we didn't take life seriously, each of us was committed to spreading joy. She taught me it was healthy to laugh at myself, and she willingly and graciously redirected my thinking when the need arose.

More to her credit, she taught me it was okay to laugh with her when she laughed at herself.

On one such occasion, Mike answered her telephone call. He turned, handing the receiver to me, and said, "It's the ding-a-ling."

Red-faced, I said timidly into the mouth piece, "Hello."

Linda responded with hysterical laughter, letting me know she had, indeed, heard Mike's words and found them to be very entertaining!

We had been reared in dissimilar faiths, but as I recall, we had only one major disagreement. Linda's children—Michelle, Cathy, and Baby Teddy—were Kristy's age (four) or younger. Linda thought I, too, needed a son. I didn't know why. Teddy Seward, full of energy, climbed out of his crib to ride his spring horse when he was supposed to be napping. He squealed loudly while chasing bugs and never seemed to stay clean.

I'd wanted to be a mother since I was four years old, and before Mike and I married, we'd agreed we wanted two little girls. God had granted the desires of our hearts. Now that Kathy and Kristy no longer needed diapers, bibs, or high chairs, I remained smug, feeling that Mike and I knew best—no more babies.

Even when my family moved, and Linda and I no longer visited daily, she stayed on Corley Street and continued to pray boldly that Mike and I would have a son.

Therefore do not be foolish, but understand what the Lord's will is. Ephesians 5:17

When Mike got orders authorizing him to finish college at government expense, we moved into the duplex Lyman had built. Mike's class schedule wasn't as hectic as the one he'd had in Kentucky. There was more time to enjoy each other and the girls.

With his uniforms packed away for several months, we were amused at the number of hometown folks who wanted to know if Mike had *finally* decided to get out of the Army. Fall arrived, and we busied ourselves raking maple leaves, riding bikes, and cleaning up the overripe yellow apples that fell from trees in our back yard. We were as comfortable as a military family could be, knowing being at home was only temporary.

We planned to go to Disney World for Christmas vacation. In the meantime, everyone in the family went to school. Mike and the girls were students, and I volunteered part-time. My dad drove the school bus that took Kathy to second grade and Kristy to kindergarten at the little country school Mike had once attended and where Mother had been office secretary.

My biggest responsibility, aside from coordinating vacation plans, seemed to be retrieving Kristy from morning kindergarten on the days I didn't volunteer. Organized and somewhat flexible, I briefly considered going back to college.

After we'd returned from Florida, but before Mike finished his education or I'd accomplished much in the volunteer work force, I learned that I did not need to look for something to fill my schedule. The baby for whom Linda had prayed was expected the week of Thanksgiving. We could almost hear God's laughter when we realized how smoothly He'd changed our plans.

Now unto him who is able to do immeasurably more than all we ask or imagine, according to his power that is at work within us, to him be glory in the church and in Christ Jesus throughout all generations, for ever and ever! Amen.
Ephesians 3:20-21

My thoughts turned to seasons of the past. Even as a young girl, when a new mother had entrusted her infant to my arms for a few minutes, I'd known my choice to become a mommy when I grew up was right. The intrigue of holding a newborn in my arms had been fostered, in part, by the fact that my cousin Larry and I were often selected to portray Joseph and Mary in our church's Christmas programs. While Larry stood at my elbow, and I held *Jesus* in my arms, I sat in awe, wondering how it might have been for Mary as she held the Christ Child. Once or twice, as I stared adoringly at the doll in "swaddling clothes," I could almost see the Baby breathing.

As the years progressed, and I actually became a mother, the longing for another baby stirred each time I held an infant, even after Mike and I had determined our family was complete. I assumed all women shared those yearnings.

Both Mike and I knew our post-war baby was a true gift from God. We humorously agreed we owed Him and His servant Linda a debt of gratitude.

While we waited, we learned Mike would not go back to Vietnam but would take his five-member family to Europe. I'd delivered neither of our daughters earlier than her due date. But I especially wanted the surprise blessing to be punctual. With those orders for West Germany hanging over my head, enjoying all the holiday season with our families loomed larger in my planning than most other years.

Truthfully, I was a bit concerned about sharing Christmas with my cousin Larry and his wife, Nancy. They'd been told by the adoption agency the wait for their baby might be months longer than Mike's and mine. I suspected having our third baby while they waited for their first might make them uncomfortable, and I was tempted to feel guilty for being so blessed.

Then, reflecting back to our childhood days, I quietly confided to my heavenly Father that this situation didn't seem fair. Respectfully, I asked Him to give Larry and Nancy a baby before we gathered to celebrate the birth of His Son. I don't remember asking more than once, but my heart remained true to its pleading.

Our Ricky was born one minute after 7:00 p.m. the Monday following Thanksgiving. Unable to sleep, Mike drove to Fort Knox, arriving on Linda's doorstep as she brewed the Tuesday morning coffee, and announced, "It's a boy!"

For the rest of the world, we printed: "Mike and Helen Jackson are proud to announce reinforcement of the Jackson family with the arrival of Trooper Richard Allen Jackson, who reported for duty on 27 Nov 72, Fort Benjamin Harrison Hospital, Indianapolis, Indiana. The new slot was allocated and does not reflect a replacement of prior personnel of this unit. Trooper Jackson at six pounds and 19 1/2 inches does not meet height and weight standards for enlistment in any other unit in the U.S. Cavalry, but really 'measures up' to family expectations!"

Within a week, we learned that Larry's and Nancy's son Kevin had been born the same minute as Ricky, and I was overwhelmed by the goodness and timing of my heavenly Father. Indeed, I was grateful Ricky had missed his due date to come the *minute* God ordained.

Mike's completion of his college education coincided with Ricky's due date, and those who issued orders graciously sent Mike back to Fort Knox for a short school.

Chapter 4

Be Strong!

Keep me safe, O God, for in you I take refuge. I said to the Lord, "You are my Lord; apart from you I have no good thing." Psalm 16:1-2

If I'd known when deciding to become a full-time military wife it might mean living on foreign soil, perhaps I would have been more resistant to the idea. As I recovered and made preliminary preparations to leave the land of my birth, I learned immunizations were required before my little family would be allowed to leave the country. When Ricky was three weeks old, his sisters and I took him, of all places, to watch us get our immunizations and to pose with us for our consolidated passport photo.

This move, unlike others, I was informed, would bring three different sets of movers--the first to pack "hold baggage" (necessities) into sturdy cardboard boxes which would travel by air; the second, less-needed personal possessions into wooden crates for slower boat travel; the third, to take everything else to storage.

Having a new baby whose daddy was home only on weekends made deciding what to take with us on the plane and what to send by air and boat difficult. Once I'd made those decisions, though, I organized our possessions by room before the movers came so that I could readily direct each stranger's attention to his share of the packing. On the mornings the movers would come, I planned to put everything going into our suitcases in the bathtub and closing the bathroom door. I'd been very trusting as a child; however, previous moves had taught me even the most experienced movers were not to be trusted. They attached no sentimental strings to my possessions, and at the time of our first move, packed Kristy's baby clothes laid aside for her suitcase into a box going on the van. And, yes, that was the move our things were delayed due to the van driver's sudden illness.

Mike finished school in time to help me watch the moving specialists. Things went well until the moving company contracted to pack "boat stuff" arrived. The younger of the two men went straight to the master bedroom, and I followed him. Mike stayed in the kitchen to watch the other one pack breakables. When my guy packed books, Mike's field boots, and baby clothes all in the same medium carton, I asked what I hope sounded like a casual question, "How long have you been working for this moving company?"

He brushed his long hair from his sparkling brown eyes, raised his eyebrows, smiled sheepishly, and answered my question with a question. "Would you believe today is my first day?"

"Really?" I asked, trying to return his smile.

"Yes," he answered. "My father-in-law owns this company, and he needed extra help today." He continued, "It's too cold for me to pour concrete this time of year. That's what I do for my regular boss--finish concrete for new swimming pools." He seemed relieved to be able to get this information off his chest. He went on, "Can't build swimming pools in February! Kim's dad needed help, and I'm here!"

My heart sank, and my face must have shown my disappointment. Pointing to his first box-packing effort, he asked, "You don't like the way I did this box, do you?" He added, "I'm real sorry I haven't had any training for packing boxes." I had to be honest; I didn't like it at all.

While he watched, I packed.

As Mike closed the door behind those two, all of my reasoning abilities vanished. My perfect moving plan had evaporated. The same temperatures which kept our mover from finishing concrete invaded the house as he went in and out to get supplies, making our home too cold for an infant. So, Ricky went to stay with Mother at the farmhouse. Looking around at our things left to go into storage, it appeared that Mike and I were now surrounded by furniture and junk we probably should have ditched. I was physically exhausted, chilled to the bone, and every tense brain cell wondered how I'd ever handle an across-the-pond crisis without family nearby. Thank goodness, Mike volunteered to supervise the next day's packing and loading of our trash and treasures.

I stood watch, making mental notes of all the things the movers (and Mike) did incorrectly. When the house was cleared of everything except uniforms, clothes, and six suitcases, we moved in with my parents.

Departure for West Germany was postponed for nearly a month because my passport was lost in the Pentagon. Mike had been issued concurrent travel orders, meaning his family would travel with him rather than wait until he was settled before joining him. He couldn't leave the U.S. until his dependents' passport was found. At first, I welcomed the opportunity to extend my time at home. But those days of waiting took their toll, as three generations sat in limbo, staring at the walls rather than looking into the eyes of the others. I could only imagine our situation was like that of a family waiting for a loved one to die.

Moses answered the people, "Do not be afraid.
Stand firm and you will see the deliverance the
Lord will bring to you today." Exodus 14:13a

Finally, Mike and I set off for West Germany late March, 1973, with three young children, leaving our mid-sized station wagon to follow us by boat. Arriving in Europe, we were left stranded for hours at the military Rhein Main airport terminal in Frankfurt. The passport delay and subsequent change in travel orders had left the personnel in Mike's unit wondering if we were ever coming to Germany. Originally, we'd been ordered to fly out of New Jersey. The cavalry squadron waiting for Mike sent a driver with a van to meet the inbound New Jersey flight. When the driver couldn't locate us, he was instructed to return the van to the motor pool. But we left from South Carolina, arriving in Frankfurt much later the same day.

While we waited for the van to return to Frankfurt for us, I walked the deserted corridors of the terminal, and my mind reflected upon our MAC (Military Air Command) flight. We'd left Charleston shortly after midnight, and every seat on the plane was occupied. As far as I knew, Ricky was the only infant on board, and his bassinet-like cardboard box we were issued kept him from falling out of his seat. His digestive tract, though, was upset by the change in water, so he didn't sleep well and spent more time in my arms than in the box.

Although I'd tried to give both of us a bath in the plane's lavatory, we were a mess. My clothing--made of that wonderful new double-knit polyester--didn't wrinkle, all right, but it carried proof Ricky's tummy was disturbed.

The stewardesses hadn't allowed us to move about the cabin, and everyone except Ricky had been required to sleep belted in and seated upright. There weren't many dependents on the flight, and it seemed all the guys had acquired the ability to *sleep anywhere*. Their snoring was deafening.

The flight bore little resemblance to civilian air travel, where the girls and I had had an abundance of help from flight attendants and had been met by either Mike or my parents when we reached our destination.

While Mike had been alone at Fort Knox, we had forwarded money and appropriate paperwork to enable an American military couple, our sponsors, to rent a German apartment, hook up utilities, and have U.S. government furniture delivered. I was greatly relieved to know the practically new, ground-floor apartment was ready for its long-overdue tenants.

By the time the military driver delivered us to our apartment in a tiny village two hours from the airport, my family was more than weary. Kathy dropped off to sleep quickly, as did Ricky, who had no trouble snuggling into his spot in one of the bedroom drawers. But Kristy, between sobs, confided to Mike and me that she hated the airplane ride, Germany, the apartment, the impromptu baby bed, *and* her bed. My take-charge husband turned to me and asked, "What are we going to do?" I suspected everything, including the dark red-on-red wall coverings and the pea green living room furniture would look better to Kristy when her eyes were rested. I prayed that I could be more objective, too.

The next morning we discovered the Pentagon wasn't the only place where something of importance could get lost. In our weariness, we'd left a huge, brown suitcase unclaimed at the airport, a suitcase we'd borrowed from Mother because we didn't prejudge accurately what needed to go with us by plane.

Upstairs, wonderful Barbara McIntosh resided with her American military pilot husband and son, Billy. As soon as she heard noises beneath her, she came down and introduced herself. She also explained that the commissary was closed every week from Saturday noon until Tuesday morning. Because we'd arrived Sunday night, she invited us up for breakfast and offered to share what she had until the next morning. She then chauffeured us into life on the East/West German border by taking us to apply for an account with the

German telephone company and on to the American school to enroll the girls in first and third grades.

While on post, Mike reported for duty and telephoned the airport, but no one there had found our missing suitcase. Consequently, I asked the Lord to find it for us. Faced with the ugly combination of wall papers and furniture, I felt I couldn't take the time to fret over one suitcase and its contents, yet I had plenty of time to roam from room to room, feeling totally helpless.

There were no built-in closets. Water tanks for toilets were overhead and to flush, one pulled on a chain. There was no "H" or "C" on the water faucets; a red dot on one handle and a blue one on the other indicated water temperatures. The space at the end of the bathtub, made for a washing machine, was too narrow for my machine. Barbara told me, though, to count it a blessing that our apartment was equipped with light fixtures and a kitchen sink--most tenants in Germany had to furnish their own. She also said my biggest adjustment initially would be that of using transformers which allowed my American appliances to run on German electrical current. Her knowledge was overwhelming; I soon considered her an expert on living in Germany.

Although government employees, our military sponsors, and Barbara tried to ease the shock of transition, I was a foreigner on the border. I didn't speak or read the local language or know the intricacies of the culture.

Mike bought a small German car for commuting while we waited for our bigger, American-made vehicle. Our hold baggage had arrived in Germany long before us, but there would be a wait, we learned, for local workers to schedule delivery. Faced with the decision to live without basics or find a way to get the large and sturdy cardboard boxes to our home, Mike signed papers accepting responsibility, discarded the boxes, and brought our things home via multiple trips in the little German car.

As soon as I passed the difficult exam which required much study but allowed me to drive abroad, Mike joined his unit in the field on maneuvers.

Each helps the other and says to his brother, "Be strong!" Isaiah 41:6

With Mike away and the children wanting to sleep while others were awake (jet lag brought on by the difference in time zones), I hesitated to send the girls to school on the bus. Nevertheless, Barbara's and my next-door neighbor, Becky, assured me I need not worry. Her David, a morning kindergartner, had had no problems.

When the girls were expected home the first day, the bus didn't appear as scheduled.

Barbara telephoned the school and learned that my daughters boarded the correct bus. But it had detoured to the American military police station, where the other parents had been encouraged to meet the driver. The purpose of the mid-afternoon meeting was to discuss a school bus incident in which an older student supposedly had tried to force drugs down the throat of a younger one.

When Barbara delivered the throat-gripping news, my flesh turned cold. I shivered as I sat waiting on the front steps, and Barbara cuddled Ricky indoors.

Chapter 5

Mine Enemy

The Lord watches over the alien . . . Psalm 146:9a

I was frantic. What could have happened? Had drugs been forced down Kathy's and Kristy's throats on their first day of school? Had the other parents taken their own children home and left mine stranded at the military police station? No matter where they were, would my daughters abandon their training and actually talk to a stranger who might help them find their way home? Was their driver the same one who'd picked them up in the morning, or was it another who couldn't be trusted?

Would Mike, the one legally responsible for us, know instinctively if his children were in danger? I imagined my two girls helpless and vulnerable, perhaps riding around the countryside, hoping to catch a glimpse of Ricky and me. They had no money, and I knew they would need to eat soon. I hoped Kathy would care for her little sister until they got back to the safety of my arms.

I'll never forget the immense relief I felt when I saw that green school bus arrive at our house. I wiped my eyes and ran to greet my children.

"Oh, I'm so glad you're home! Am I happy to see you!" I exclaimed.

The bus driver nodded, apparently in agreement, and pulled away.

Kathy, with the same hands-on-hips posture she'd taken at Fort Hood, declared, "I know my time clock is off, but this

49

day of third grade was too long!" She continued, "Is dinner ready?"

I looked at my tiny and delicately featured first grader. It appeared that Kristy didn't have a clue that she'd been separated from her mother for ten hours. She said nothing as I hugged her tenderly.

Kathy continued, "Kristy should be rested. She's been asleep ever since we left the police station."

As I opened the heavy front door, I asked, "Oh? Why were you at the police station?"

"Some big kid got in trouble, I think."

"Do you know why?" I asked, hoping against hope that the school secretary who'd talked to Barbara had been mistaken.

"Well, I'm not real sure, but there were a lot of people yelling at each other. You know how upset Grandpa gets when someone on his bus uses bad words." She continued, stopping only to catch her breath, "I think the big boy must have called the little boy a bad name."

I decided not to pursue the subject any further. It was time for dinner, but I had no appetite.

I learned later that when Mr. Bus Driver, who spoke very little English, finished his evening route, ready to return the bus to post, he found two small blue-eyed passengers who spoke no German sitting between him and his vehicle's rear emergency door.

He sought the help of the Thorntons, an American military family, who lived two towns away and spoke both his and my daughters' languages. Hannah, the eighth-grade student in the home, remembered observing the girls board the bus with David, our next-door kindergartner, that morning. She reminded her bus driver that normally he did not travel our street on his evening route and directed him to our location.

After my children had gone to bed, I reviewed all the *what ifs* that had crossed my mind during the two hours of not knowing my children's' whereabouts. None of those horrible things I'd imagined came to be. I knew that by the time Mike returned, my fears would sound silly, even to me. Having observed my daddy care for children as their bus driver, I was certain there was a loving wife nearby listening to her husband tell of his rotten work day and gently assuring him that his tomorrow would be better.

Understanding things were totally out of my control, I knew I had to trust God in our new surroundings. He reminded me that He had taken care of me when I was a little girl and assured me He loved my daughters more than I loved them. Even so, I wrote Linda Seward, my Corley Street friend, that if she were offered the opportunity to come live in my new town, to pass it up.

I looked around. Things really would be better once Mike came home, the telephone was functioning, the landlord put in a lawn, and our car and other things arrived by boat.

. . . for your Father knows what you need before you ask him. Matthew 6:8b

Only a couple of months after Mike returned and our second shipment was settled in, friends we'd met at Fort Knox came to live next door. Soon those friends were notified they would sponsor Linda's family to come to our area! I had heard other wives at Fort Knox say that you never truly have to say good-bye in military circles because someone will always be at your next post to greet you.

Before my joyful friend and her family arrived, Mike's mother telephoned to announce the brown suitcase had been delivered to her home in Indiana. We never learned why it was easier to have the suitcase retrace its route to Indiana than to have it delivered to Mike, only two hours from the Frankfurt airport!

The one thing I could explain was the disappearance of my postnatal flab. Each load of laundry had to be carried from the basement to the third-floor attic, where clothes lines were strung from end to end. Once up the pull-down ladder that gave me access to the attic, I opened the windows for cross ventilation and hung up the heavy, wet clothes to dry. On many of those trips I carried Ricky on my back.

Kathy and Kristy began learning German by playing with Petra from down the street. Each girl took turns being the teacher. If Kathy pointed to a doll, she'd say, "Doll." Then Petra repeated, "Doll." When she was confident that she had learned the English word, she'd say, "Puppe," (pronounced POO-pa) and Kristy and Kathy repeated the German word until they, too, were confident they'd mastered it.

Mike and I took a night class on post to learn the language.

He sends from heaven and saves me, rebuking those who hotly pursue me; God sends his love and his faithfulness. Psalm 57:3

One of the most frustrating things about my introductory language course was it taught me how to find food, transportation, and shelter, but not how to communicate with school bus drivers and appliance repairmen. When my very old and yellowed one-door refrigerator refused to let me inside to prepare lunch one day, I called those in charge of maintenance and asked them to help me open the refrigerator door.

That afternoon a repairman came to the village from post. He pulled on the big handle, just as I had done, with the same results. He looked at his work order and then at me. With anger spewing from every pore, he waved his arms and stomped to my telephone.

Following a short conversation I couldn't understand, he forcefully returned the telephone receiver to its rightful place and stormed back into the kitchen. With his hammer, he pried the door open, completely destroying the latch. As he shoved a pen into my one hand and his work order into the other, I was afraid not to sign on the line, indicating I was pleased with his solution.

After days of untying one end of the rope he'd knotted around the broken handle and looped around the refrigerator coils, I was pleasantly surprised when he returned with a newer refrigerator. His younger, English-speaking helper explained that the refrigerator assigned to me had been swapped, without proper paperwork, for the antiquated one whose door now couldn't be repaired. That's why he'd been so angry! Unsuspecting Helen had been suspected of selling government property! Once I understood, I was able to smile in two languages.

If it is possible, as far as it depends on you, live at peace with everyone. Romans 12:18

American troops were away on maneuvers or patrolling the East/West German border almost as often as they were home. After six months in the village, as a matter of economy (we could sell the smaller car) and practicality (Mike could spend more time with his wife and children), the Jacksons moved to a stairwell apartment on post.

Surrounded by American women and their children, I wanted all of us to be one big, happy family. But a couple of the wives who'd been there much longer than I had had their fill of single parenting, cramped quarters, and depleted finances. They wanted their husbands to come home more often than duty allowed. Taking their cares upon myself, I wavered between wanting to help each one and wanting to run from them all. Not knowing how to help, whenever Mike came home, I unloaded on him all their frustrations I'd gathered like a little vacuum cleaner, as well as some of my own.

When he'd reached his fill of my dumping, he sent the children and me back to Indiana for an extended summer vacation.

I didn't know I needed a change of scenery until I handed my passport to the agent in New York. He looked at my document and then into my eyes.

"Welcome home, Mrs. Jackson," he said quietly.

I began weeping.

Even though I knew Jesus had not forsaken me, even though Linda and her family now lived in my building and the German folk I'd met were wonderful, the fact remained that West Germany wasn't home. But I was on my way home! A quick bath for my toddler who'd cried all the way across the ocean, a jump onto another plane, and in a flash, I'd be back on the farm. The girls wanted something to eat, but I told them that we were scheduled to have dinner on the next flight. They could wait.

We boarded the flight for Indy. When the children were belted in with pillows and blankets, I slipped off my shoes and let my head fall back against the seat, closing my eyes. It was the wee hours of the morning in Germany, and wrestling with Ricky as he cried had exhausted me.

I awakened to the voice of the Captain telling his passengers that the 45-minute wait we'd had on the ground was due to a mechanical failure. He apologized for the lack of circulating air, then instructed us to deplane, get a voucher for dinner, and check back at the gate in two hours.

While the other passengers began to get off the aircraft, I took stock: one umbrella stroller, two shoes that didn't want

to go back on my feet, three sleeping children, and three
carryon bags.

I shook Kathy's shoulder, "Kathy, I need your help." No
response. "Kris, I need for you to wake up." No response. But
Ricky woke up immediately and began to complain loudly that
he needed a drink.

After everyone else had left the plane, a stewardess came
back to our seats over the left wing and asked, "Is there a
problem?" I explained why I was having difficulty complying
with the Captain's instructions, and asked if she could just slip
our dinner vouchers into the side pocket of my bag while I
awakened my children.

"Oh," she looked somewhat ill at ease, "since you bought
only one adult ticket, I can only let you have one five-dollar
voucher. The children don't qualify. Perhaps you could share
with them." She excused herself and went back toward the
cockpit. Shortly, the overhead lights in the plane went out.

I'm not sure how I managed to get my shoes back on, and
all of us off the darkened plane, and to purchase a snack and
drink. I tried to call my folks, but they'd already left home for
Indianapolis. At that point we decided it would be better for
us, as tired as we were, to go to the corner of the gate area
and try to rest.

Two hours later a brave ticket agent made his way through
the crowd of grumpy passengers to the microphone and
announced, "Folks, we're really sorry, but we can't repair this
plane. Please report to Gate 15 on the fourth concourse. It's
about a ten-minute walk, and your flight will leave there in
about an hour. We apologize for the delay." I guess he wasn't
too brave, after all, because he disappeared very quickly. The
passengers, most of whom were now muttering, slowly began
making their way to the other gate.

Kathy said, "Mom, I'm sorry, but I can't carry this bag
anywhere."

Kristy, on the other hand, decided to take things into her own hands. She marched over to a airline employee who was driving an electric cart, and asked, "Would you please take us to Gate 15?"

"Yes, just as soon as I take this couple who can't walk, I'll come back for you." He drove away.

As the crowd thinned, I saw another mother with as many bags as she had kids, and I asked her if she'd like to wait and ride with us. She did. We waited as the clock ticked away. When the man who'd promised Kristy a ride didn't return, I found another employee pushing a broom and asked if there was any way I could contact the other man to come back for us.

"Oh, I don't think so. You see, those carts have to go back for recharging at ten p.m."

Nearly in tears, the other mom asked, "Where do you keep the wheel chairs?" Taking pity on us, he brought two wheelchairs, and helped us load up all the luggage, her kids, and my girls onto the chairs. He then pushed one of the chairs so I, barefoot by now, could push sleeping Ricky's stroller.

Separated from Mike and his duty station by the Atlantic Ocean, I realized I'd left Europe cynical and critical. Somehow I'd have to remember not everything in the U.S. is perfect and that our living in Germany was temporary. I'd remember this night and return to my husband in a better frame of mind.

Finally on the farm, I rested. As always, Mother took her job as hostess very seriously. She and Daddy had put a swimming pool in their side yard and dragged down toys from upstairs. They'd made arrangements for old school friends to come play with Kathy and Kristy.

One day, Mother asked, "Is there anything you'd especially like to have to eat while you're here?"

"Donuts!" we said in unison. German food was wonderful, but I'd found the pastries to be much less sweet and moist than those I'd grown to love as a child.

Mother wasn't amused when the children and I consumed all the donuts she'd purchased for the evening's dessert and the next day's breakfast in one afternoon sitting.

Again, the big, brown suitcase left Indiana by air. This time it carried fabric, patterns, and other things we'd needed in Europe and hadn't found (no donuts, though).

Linda laughed as she looked over the treasures I'd brought back from the States. Stamped on the package of the needles I'd purchased for my American sewing machine were the words, "Made in West Germany."

No sooner were the girls back in school for the fall session than I learned one of the four-bedroom sets of quarters would be vacant in September, one month before Kathy turned ten. She looked forward to this particular birthday, knowing it meant she'd not only get her own I.D. card but also, under Army regulations, would qualify for her own bedroom.

There were no families on the four- or three-bedroom waiting lists. A mother of one toddler girl announced publicly that since their name was at the top of the two-bedroom list, they'd soon move to the big apartment.

My intentions to live in peace with all flew out the floor-to-ceiling balcony door.

Privately, I telephoned the housing office to see if it were a fact that this family of three would move into a four-bedroom apartment while my family of five continued to be crunched into one with three bedrooms. Mrs. Grimes, the secretary with a pleasant-sounding voice, verified that there were no names on any waiting list except the two-bedroom one. She went on to tell me if there were a family who would soon qualify for the bigger apartment, the military member of that family should scoot right down to her office with birth certificates.

From the very beginning of Mike's career, I'd made it a policy not to call him during duty hours. Not only was it rude to interrupt his work, but also he agreed I was competent to handle things at home. He knew, however, if he received a message to call home during duty hours, it was very important.

Immediately after I hung up from talking to Mrs. Grimes, the government employee who'd just become my best friend, I called Mike's workplace. Mike himself answered. With urgency in my voice, I said, "Please come home for lunch," and hung up. I didn't want anyone else listening through our front door and hearing my plan of action.

The walk from Mike's work station to his quarters normally took him about four minutes. I'd barely opened our blue metal Important Papers box, when Mike breathlessly opened the door and asked, "What's wrong?"

I explained that if we waited until Kathy's birthday to ask for a bigger apartment, the almost vacant quarters would be gone. In addition, there were no more projected openings until the next spring.

My wonderful husband immediately got in the car with his tuna salad sandwich and drove to see Mrs. Grimes and arrange for Kathy's birthday surprise.

Mission accomplished. I didn't even care that, while Mike and his unit were in the field, I'd have to move and put everything away in the new quarters and clear the old ones by myself.

And the God of all grace, who called you to his eternal glory in Christ, after you have suffered a little while, will himself restore you and make you strong, firm and steadfast. To him be the power for ever and ever. Amen. I Peter 5:10-11

"Army brat," commonly used to identify a kid reared in military communities, was a term I found distasteful. First of all, Mike and I didn't want any of our children to display brat-like behavior. Secondly, I felt it was a degrading title for such a plucky part of our society. Others, I learned, felt the term was endearing, indicating those who'd learned to be super-resilient.

The girls were allowed to go almost anywhere on post except the areas where the single soldiers lived. They walked to the Girl Scout Hut and the exchange, or to meet their friends on any of the playgrounds. Ricky (now two) was pretty much restricted to the stairwell and the lawn directly behind our quarters. Fortunately, two-year-old Tommy lived next door and became Ricky's buddy. Unfortunately, what one little boy didn't think of, the other did.

One day shortly after the one during which the little guys took off their jeans and shirts and threw them into the big dumpster, I couldn't find Ricky. I asked Tommy's mother, Judy, if she knew the boys' whereabouts. She thought they were with me. We didn't allow the boys to cross the street in front of our building, so we mothers went toward the back where the boys often played under the tall pine trees. They were not behind our building.

When we found that they had not only crossed the street, but were playing in the post commander's garage, Judy and I were mortified. We apologized profusely for our sons having interrupted her solitude, and the apologies were graciously accepted. Later, we learned that Tommy and Ricky had not only played that day but several others, each time knocking on the nice lady's door to announce their arrival. Too late, we learned it was usually when the nice lady was trying to rest! At that point, we wondered if *our* sons had ever been called "Army brats."

*Let your eyes look straight ahead, fix your gaze
directly before you. Make level paths for your feet
and take only ways that are firm. Do not swerve to
the right or to the left; keep your foot from evil.*
Proverbs 4:25-27

By 1975, we were well into the last half of the 38-month
overseas assignment when the wives and children of Mike's
unit were invited to tour the border camp where our husbands
and fathers spent three-week working rotations while their
families remained on post. The American soldier who served
as our guide asked mothers to take the hands of their children
so none of them would accidentally wander into unfriendly
territory. He pointed out the zones along the border and
explained some of the duties of American personnel who
worked there.

The longer he talked, the tighter Kristy's grip on my hand
became. Only nine years old, she already understood the
possibility of getting into a situation where neither her parents
nor her government could help her.

Hearing a U.S. soldier describe the consequences for one
of us straying across the border or any East German trying to
escape to the West (they'd be killed) was only slightly less
sobering than my trip into the observation tower. I was
handed a pair of binoculars and told to look in the direction of
the tower on the opposite side of the border. My binoculars
locked onto those of an East German border guard. How can
one describe the wisdom and understanding that comes from
being face to face with the enemy? Instantly, I knew why Mike
had always said, "This is a profession, not a job." There,
perhaps more than most other assignments, America's
professional, self-sacrificing soldiers longed for peace while
they uniquely filled the gap between dreams of peace and the
reality of being peacekeepers.

With the sudden influx of knowledge, I experienced a fleeting moment of mistrust. Personally, I had no mistrust of the soldier into whose eyes I stared, yet my intellect told me I should. Fences, mine fields, and formal declarations between our countries made the young man my enemy.

Praise the Lord, O my soul; all my inmost being, praise his holy name. Praise the Lord, O my soul, and forget not all his benefits. He forgives all my sins and heals all my diseases; he redeems my life from the pit and crowns me with love and compassion. He satisfies my desires with good things, so that my youth is renewed like the eagle's. Psalm 103:1-5

For the first time in my life, I consciously experienced freedom.

I left the border camp grateful for having been born in the United States and with a new appreciation of Mike's commitment. I pledged to proudly carry my identification card I'd once thought took away my individuality, and to become more tolerant of the time Mike spent defending us and our allies. Meanwhile, I knew his meals would continue to dry out in our oven while he followed orders and tended to the younger soldiers' health and welfare.

For God so loved the world that he gave his one and only Son, that whoever believes in him shall not perish but have eternal life. God did not send his Son into the world to condemn the world, but to save the world through him. John 3:16-17

*But I tell you: Love your enemies and pray for those
who persecute you.* Matthew 5:44

On another day in another place, reality of the East
German's and my meeting became more focused. If I
understood my *New Testament* correctly, Jesus came to save,
not condemn, both the solemn-faced German and the
American woman who knew freedom. As a young girl, I'd
known how important it was to do what Jesus asked of me--to
be obedient. I'd sung the words, "I'll go where you want me
to go, dear Lord." But I'd whispered the request, "Please
don't ask me to be a missionary."

While in Germany, I was, to the best of my ability,
answering the call to serve my unseen but so very real God,
half-way around the world from the farm. Yet, I had to
confess to Him that any prayer for the enemy I'd seen had
stuck in my throat.

Was the man married? Did he have children? Did he
experience periods of loneliness while he stood watch? Did he
allow the memories of his childhood to trigger homesickness?

I now had to consider whether the enemies the Bible
instructed me to love and pray for were these young people
who lived half-a-world away and worked in the same
profession as my husband.

*Cast your bread upon the waters, for after many
days you will find it again.* Ecclesiastes 11:1

Linda and I cochaired a community bazaar, working many
hours to plan and coordinate with German vendors who
wanted to sell their wares to Americans. Monies the wives'
club reaped from our volunteer hours funded scholarships and

underbudgeted post activities. Working with Linda as if we were business partners made the project extremely rewarding. With these and other events, our time in Germany came to an end. As Mike and I prepared to leave the country, we purchased a European station wagon reputed to be very safe, though somewhat small and extremely ugly by my standards. When it arrived, we sold our American car to an Air Force family who'd be staying in Europe a few more years. Then we ordered three rooms of furniture from catalogues. The saleslady assured us our purchases would wait patiently in North Carolina for us until we were settled at our next stateside post.

Before Mike, the children, and I headed to Frankfurt for our flight home, we went to see the new baby in our building. Linda and family had named her Annemarie. Mike tenderly picked up the newborn and retreated to a rocking chair in the corner of her living room. If anyone else offered or asked to hold Annemarie, Mike replied, "She's just fine where she is."

Linda's prayers had come full circle. She'd thought perhaps she wanted another baby but had been told that was not probable. For the brief moment Mike let me snuggle Annemarie, I realized my former stirring for another baby had dissipated with Ricky's birth. Yet, sharing Linda's joy of knowing both our families were completed in God's timing warmed me, even as the tears streaming down my cheeks reminded me Linda's family wouldn't follow us to our next post. I would have no part in Annemarie's nurturing.

Chapter 6

Love Does No Harm

Love does no harm to its neighbor. Romans 13:10a

While combat unit assignments usually eat up most of the free time of military men, those who've been around very long observe those assignments being interrupted by military schools and projects that may or may not be related to the serviceman's primary job skill. Most guys with families, even if they don't like school, appreciate long school assignments that allow families to regroup and enjoy each other's company.

When we left the "Cav" unit in Germany in 1976, Mike was assigned to Warren, Michigan (a Detroit suburb), to work on a project that would eventually add a new tank to the nation's arsenal. I was told to expect Mike to work normal hours. When he scouted the new environment, he learned his office was next door to a shopping mall; he would wear civilian business attire; and the only post in the area was a national guard base whose quarters were too small for us and our new furniture.

On the third day of our searching for a civilian home closer to the shopping center than the military base, the realtor asked if we'd consider living in a condominium. I told him I would, but in my mind I associated common walls and staircases with the tight communal living I'd just eagerly left. I was comfortable with military neighbors and their moving in and out. Looking for a civilian place to live, I suspected finding good neighbors might not be easy. Also, if I got a bad one, and she stayed as long as I, this assignment might seem longer than three years. But once we'd looked at the condo the realtor had in mind for us, it appeared to me that the Kleppers were just the people we *needed* for next-door neighbors.

Although out of character for both of us, Mike and I returned without the realtor, approaching Gus and Betty Klepper to ask if they liked the area. It was obvious not many who'd looked at the condo had stopped by to chat with the dignified older couple. They assured us they thought the complex would be a good place to rear children.

Almost as soon as we'd signed the "Offer to Purchase," it became apparent Mike's newest responsibilities would cause him to travel several days a week. So much for the normal work schedule. Until we could take possession of our condo, the children and I stayed with my folks, who'd left the farmhouse for a newer but smaller home.

Mike came to us on weekends. While he traveled, the girls and Daddy took Ricky to the farm to experience with him the "fun stuff" we'd all done in times past. While they played, Mother and I drank coffee at her dining room table, allowing me to adjust quietly to the house my parents now called home. Once our four shipments of personal belongings and furniture were delivered to the condo, my folks, who'd brought the children and me to Michigan and stayed to help, traveled the six hours back home.

I soon discovered a problem. The company that had contracted to keep our things safely in storage failed to deliver, among other things, the swing set Grandpa Garner (Mother's dad) had designed and fabricated for my seventh birthday. To be honest, the iron pipe, cross irons, hand-crafted wooden seats, and old chains probably had little intrinsic value. To anyone else, the swing set would have looked like junk. But in my heart, the U.S. government had betrayed me by allowing inept people to handle my treasure.

Both condo association rules and limited patio space prohibited our erecting a swing set. But I longed to awaken some morning and discover my disassembled swing set on my front doorstep. Mike didn't seem to appreciate the extent of my loss, and I could find no other government employee who cared to listen to my grievance. Even the personnel of the insurance company who'd readily accepted our premium payments, weren't swayed by my pleas for help.

When I learned I would be the one doing the leg work needed to create a paper trail to prove my losses and validate their worth, I was angry. Nevertheless, I slowly began collecting evidence of purchase and replacement costs. Then I began the tedious process of filling out the paper work for both the government and our insurance company.

If I'd known then what I know now, I'd have spent my time more wisely, finding a way to get inside the storage facility to recover the swing set, Mike's tools and tool boxes, and our walnut coffee table!

Whether I needed our European car or not, when Mike traveled by plane, I felt better knowing I could escape the condo if I wanted. For that reason, I often drove Mike to and from the Detroit airport. Otherwise, that foreign station wagon sat in the airport parking lot, smack-dab in the middle of the land of the Big Three auto makers. But one good thing about having a unique vehicle in a huge metropolitan airport parking lot--Mike could easily find his car!

After the stairwell living of Germany, where I'd been surrounded by multitudes of other young families, and having visited with my relatives for six weeks, I found myself in Michigan feeling very isolated and lonely. I hesitated to ask the Kleppers for help as I might have done if they'd been military. I reasoned they'd reared their five children and earned a rest. Yet, the other neighbors ignored my children and me, and I knew no other military families in the area. The national guard base was 28 miles from us in the opposite direction of the airport, but I went there for commissary shopping and to drink in any sense of home that I could find.

I missed Linda and the comradery of stairwell living. I needed Betty's friendship, and once I expressed that need, she began to share wisdom and friendship with me as if I were a part of her family.

Have mercy on me, O God, have mercy on me, for in you my soul takes refuge. I will take refuge in the shadow of your wings until the disaster has passed.
Psalm 57:1

Just when I thought I'd reached a point in my life when I could be adept at motherhood and handling crisis situations, Ricky, age three, began to limp. His foot wasn't bruised, nor were his shoes too short.

The problem began less than a month after we'd moved into the condo. Away from military medical care, I asked Betty to recommend a good local pediatrician. When I called for an appointment, the secretary didn't ask me for Mike's social security number right away as someone from a military hospital would have. Instead, she wanted to know how many days my son had limped and what kind of insurance we had. The more questions I answered, the more it dawned on me that it might take a long time to get a new-patient appointment.

Finally, she told me I could bring Ricky to see the doctor the very next week. I asked, "Do you know any other good pediatricians who take new patients?"

Obviously taken aback by my boldness, she asked, "Is Ricky your firstborn?"

"No, he's the youngest of three."

"Can you come in day after tomorrow at one?"

The pediatrician wasn't an alarmist. After thoroughly examining Ricky, he decided not to order X-rays, convinced the deep muscular discomfort would pass within ten days. He advised me to watch Ricky closely and to carry him if he asked to be.

Instead of improving, the limping worsened, and Ricky began to complain of pain. He stumbled into walls as he navigated the condo's three levels. He awakened at night, wanting one of us to come to his room to comfort him.

Even though the doctor was preparing to leave for vacation, he made space in his work schedule for us. This time he turned to me, his eyes speaking regret and his voice quivering.

"Hip disease is ugly. I'll send you to the hospital for X-rays and call the best orthopedic surgeon I know."

Peace I leave with you; my peace I give you. I do not give to you as the world gives. Do not let your hearts be troubled and do not be afraid. John 14:27

Early in our marriage Mike had been troubled when I cried for what he considered no reason. Truly, I'd cried often. Kathy's and Kristy's tears unnerved him, as well. But the morning following the doctor's visit, as Mike and I held our son's hands in the emergency room and Ricky begged to leave the scary sights and sounds surrounding him, it was Mike who shed tears.

My parents came quickly, and during the next five days, I wept quietly when I could be alone. Waiting to hear just how bad the bad news could be was one of the most difficult things I'd been forced to do. Food had no taste. My normally soothing bed pillow was lumpy beyond belief. Minor frustrations and disappointments mushroomed into catastrophes as we waited for the medical experts' consolidated opinion.

While ten-year-old Kristy, too young to visit Ricky in the hospital, waited at home, she struggled with thoughts she'd occasionally entertained toward her pesky little brother. Kleppers, grandparents, and parents rallied to support Kristy's broken heart and dispel the unwarranted fear that she could have done something to prevent Ricky's misfortune.

Confined to a hospital bed, Ricky explained his only need quite frankly--if Mother and I would leave the hospital room, "us guys" (Ricky and Grandpa) could play.

After days of testing, we learned Ricky's hip wasn't diseased. Instead, his left femur contained a bone cyst (hole) just below the top growth plate. He was bound in an extensive plaster cast and sent home.

Undoubtedly there since birth, the weakened spot had probably fractured once Ricky was old enough to escape his mother's watchful eye for more than a couple of minutes. The doctors told Mike and me recovery might take a long time. God's mercy prevented me from suspecting the specialist spoke of years, not weeks or months, for the hole to fill in with new bone.

Although we were practically isolated from our military family, word of our need for support spread with unbelievable speed. Cards and letters poured in, assuring us we were swaddled in others' thoughts and prayers.

The resourcefulness I'd gained through years of making the best of my circumstances proved very helpful in designing clothing to fit over Ricky's cumbersome cast and in structuring family activities around a boy who couldn't bend at the waist. The cast started at his chest; his hips, left leg, and the upper half of his right leg were locked into place at about a 45-degree angle.

Determined not to stay home and feel sorry for ourselves, we bought a sturdy children's wagon. Its removable sides and ends made it easy for us to convert the toy into a very comfortable form of transportation for Ricky. We learned that a child in hardened plaster, though, should not spend a day at the Detroit zoo! Ricky had worn a brimmed cap and sunglasses. We'd made sure he had plenty to drink. But we did not think about the cast absorbing heat. By the time we headed for home, Ricky was ill. Even though he recovered quickly, I could see the headlines: "Local Lad Roasts at Zoo."

Everywhere we went, folks looked at Ricky with great sadness in their eyes. Children with no inhibitions came up to ask, "What happened?" Like Kristy, I looked at that cast and wondered what I could have done to prevent Ricky's broken leg.

At the end of ten weeks, Ricky went back to the hospital. All he cared about was his expected freedom. I wanted to know the fracture was healed. Just as he'd allowed me to stay with Ricky when the cast went on, Resident Simmons allowed me to observe its coming off.

The sight and sound of the blade headed for his chest and abdomen didn't faze Ricky, but I cringed at the noise and mess the procedure produced. First, Dr. Simmons made a slit on each side of the cast from Ricky's armpits to his toes and then on the inside at the same distance from the table. Within five minutes from the time he'd begun, Dr. Simmons removed the top half, exposing Ricky's pale, scaling skin. Tenderly, the doc eased Ricky out of the bottom half of the cast so that the cyst area could be X-rayed. Dr. Simmons explained that if the fracture wasn't healed to orthopedic satisfaction, he'd place Ricky back between the two hardened pieces of plaster, taping them back together for another few weeks.

I prayed, "Oh God, please." Our heavenly Father knew the rest of my prayer and had already answered. Ricky went home with instructions not to put weight on the left foot. Any pressure on the weakened bone might fracture the mended femur once more. Worse yet, if it splintered, the fragments of bone might damage the growth plate and cause permanent impairment. Mike and I carried Ricky wherever he needed to go.

A few weeks later, I took Ricky back to see the doctor at his office. The seasoned nurse asked me how long I felt my back would survive the strain of carrying my child everywhere. I hadn't given my back one thought. Now that she brought it to my attention, I realized her concern had a double meaning. I had yet to acknowledge the likely time frame of Ricky's recovery; I could injure myself seriously if I continued to carry him.

She asked the doctor to prescribe an adjustable strap that would cross Ricky's chest, encircle his waist, and hang down behind his left knee. A metal hook attached to the bottom end would snap to the heel of a sturdy left shoe, keeping Ricky's foot up and his toes pointing toward the ground. It sounded simple, but everything had to be custom made, and the coordination of all the measuring and ordering was my job. It was over a month later, in therapy, that Ricky learned to walk on his right foot with the aid of a very small pair of crutches. Seeing him wobble and list from side to side, all the while smiling proudly, made me realize that our son wouldn't be held back from living life to its fullest.

We knew it was potentially dangerous for Ricky, as curious as most four-year-olds, to be left alone. But we also understood that he must be allowed some freedom to be the boy he was designed to be. Ricky was enrolled in school and bussed to a special classroom, a protected environment where no one would bump into him. I was truly relieved he was in capable hands while I took a much-needed break from caring for him 24 hours a day.

I was physically tired from being my son's care-giver and welcomed the professional help that his teacher, Miss Tosetti, her aides, and the bus driver gave. But that first morning I missed my little sidekick, whose temporary handicap had totally consumed me. During the early weeks, I'd consistently acknowledged my need for God's help while I practiced appearing as if the care I gave Ricky was nothing more important than washing his clothes. As his nurse, I followed doctors' orders carefully while I tried to keep my emotions from leaping onto my face. This desire to show Ricky only my courage and love, not pity, was more noble that the temptation I'd had on many occasions to try to hide my insecurities from other adults. Ricky needed new horizons; I needed some quiet time.

After two days in Miss Tosetti's classroom, Easter break arrived. While away from his protected environment, Ricky stumbled, fracturing the bone, and began another twelve-week period of plastered immobility.

I was dejected. Only two days and it looked as if Ricky's pre-school days had ended. By the time he'd be able to walk with crutches again, the school year would be over. I called the district's transportation department to inform them of Ricky's accident and thank them for the two days they'd served us. I nearly jumped up and down when I learned Ricky would be picked up as usual. His red wagon would be loaded via the lift and chained to the bus frame for safe travel.

Again the break mended, and we entered Ricky in swimming classes to strengthen his arm and leg muscles. It was in his *real* school classroom, though, that Ricky Jackson fell in love for the first time. I had to agree, giving his heart to Miss Tosetti set a great precedent. She was genuinely kind, very pretty, and a willing vessel in the hands of the Master Potter.

Less than a year later, Ricky tripped and broke his leg again. This time, the fracture required traction.

O Lord, I call to you; come quickly to me. Hear my voice when I call to you. May my prayer be set

*before you like incense; may the lifting up of my
hands be like the evening sacrifice.* Psalm 141:1-2

Some would say Ricky was in the right place at the right
time or that he was lucky. In 1978, he was the third child in
the Detroit area to receive a new treatment for cysts such as
his. Although very effective, the treatment wasn't an instant
cure. Nevertheless, I knew our being associated with the
nearby world-reknowned doctors was not a coincidence but a
gift from our heavenly Father.

By the time of the fourth casting in 1981, we'd left
Michigan, gone to school for a year in Kansas, and were in the
second year of another Fort Hood assignment. As a result of
the fracture and a season of traction in the hospital, Rick
recovered at home and was tutored for one semester of fourth
grade. Even though his body was bigger and I needed more
equipment to lift, turn, and move him, I rested in the
knowledge that Rick's growth plate in that leg had never been
damaged.

At the time of that fracture, both girls attended high school;
Mike's mother, Margaret, lived with us; and I'd just failed at a
business venture. Even though I was better experienced at
sharing my compassion and encouragement than I had been
during the earlier assignment to Fort Hood, I had no energy
for helping those outside my four walls.

I resented anyone associated with the Army asking me for
help. I felt as if no one else at Fort Hood understood (or
attempted to learn) the strain and demands on my time as I
struggled to be "all things to all people."

When Rick returned to elementary school, I joined the
other moms who worked outside the home, and Margaret
settled back in Indiana.

Do not be anxious about anything, but in everything,
by prayer and petition, with thanksgiving, present
your requests to God. And the peace of God, which
transcends all understanding, will guard your hearts
and minds in Christ Jesus. Philippians 4:6-7

Even though the Lord delivered me from most of the fears
I'd dragged with me into adulthood, one continued to nag at
me. I fretted I wouldn't be able to get back to Indiana quickly
from a far-away post if one of my parents needed me.
Wherever we lived, they'd always been available when one of
us needed comfort or an extra pair of hands. I wanted to do
the same for them.

Just as precisely as the Lord gave two handsome baby boys
in one minute, He eradicated my long-standing concerns.

As the third Thanksgiving season of the Fort Hood
assignment approached, I wanted to go back to Indiana for my
turkey dinner. The intense longing confounded me;
nevertheless, Mike urged me to go, if for no other reason than
I might be homesick. Mother arranged a family potluck so I
could visit with my grandma, Daddy's two brothers, and their
families.

Although still weak from a recent stay in the cardiac unit of
the hospital, Aunt June (Cousin Larry's mother) arrived ready
to have a good time. The official family photographer, she
took many snapshots. As we parted, she told me she loved me
and promised to send me prints if her photos turned out well. I
don't remember her telling me she loved me before that night,
but I'm confident she had. From my early childhood, her
actions, not the least of which was catering Mike's and my
wedding, consistently assured me of her love.

Before bedtime, Aunt June went to be with Jesus, leaving
me with awe of having been summoned more than 1,000 miles
to share her last fun-filled day.

No longer confused by my yearnings for Thanksgiving in Indiana, I walked away from the shackles of my fear and trusted the Holy Spirit to keep me on the right path and in His timing, no matter where Mike's orders took me.

Chapter 7

Delight Yourself in the Lord

Do not withhold your mercy from me, O Lord; may your love and your truth always protect me. Psalm 40:11

Since our days at Fort Knox, I'd held the theory that if Military Mom adjusted, Military Dad had the energy he needed to adjust to his new assignment. Furthermore, if Mom adjusted and Dad got off on the right foot, the kids, extroverted or not, found friends and flourished. When given the opportunity, my children seemed to develop friendships with both Army brats and civilians.

When we learned in 1983 that we were headed for Europe once again, Kathy, having graduated from high school, decided she would marry and not go with us. I was confident that Mario, an Army brat whose father was retired, would be a good husband. I was at peace with their decision, yet I knew leaving Kathy behind might be one of the most difficult things I'd ever do. Even the thought of leaving her behind was painful. I had to ask myself if my theory about adjusting would remain valid once an ocean separated Kathy and me.

Two weeks before the wedding, Mike was alerted he'd be needed in Europe in a matter of weeks, not months. The change in plans meant he'd begin immediately to out-process (the drill of disassociating himself from one unit to transfer to another). So, from the Army's point of view, all of the Jacksons would leave Ft. Hood for Germany ASAP.

What they didn't know was that I was still engulfed in wedding preparations, Kristy would graduate from high school in a few months, and our house would have to sell during the winter. For the first time in our lives we had to consider the needs of our family as well as the needs of the Army. Mike and I made a decision that he would go to Europe alone for six months, and I'd continue to carry on alone with the plans we'd made before Mike's orders were changed. Furthermore, we agreed that neither of us would accept guilt from others for doing what we knew was right.

As Mike, in his dress uniform, escorted Mario's bride down the aisle of the church, I stood in amazement. I'd never seen Mike look more handsome, nor his daughter more beautiful. All eyes focused on the two of them while the Lord privately lubricated the workings of my heart with joy.

So, if you think you are standing firm, be careful you don't fall! No temptation has seized you except what is common to man. And God is faithful; he will not let you be tempted beyond what you can bear. But when you are tempted, he will also provide a way out so that you can stand up under it.
I Corinthians 10:12-13

When we'd left Europe the first time, I'd made a bold statement, "I'm not coming back here without my own furniture."

Others who knew that was not the way the system worked asked me, "How are you going to do that?"

I didn't have an answer; I simply knew the folks who'd selected the sturdy upholstery fabric got a good deal on large shipments of pea green, mustard yellow, and dirt brown. By the time I'd looked at them in every single American home we'd visited for three years, I was sick of looking at all three colors. The only relief each family had from their quarters looking like everyone else's was the pictures and bric-a-brac they'd brought from the States or purchased in Germany.

This time, during a period when the government didn't have much furniture to distribute, we were allowed to take all ours with us. I thanked the Lord that He continued to hear my heart. Not only would I get to live with all my things, but also my American dollars would purchase more Deutsche marks than the last time we'd lived in West Germany.

Kristy, Rick, Spunky (our Sheltie), and I joined Mike in stages following Kristy's graduation in May. We found very quickly that our little quarters were a bit crowded. We'd have to use a corner of Kristy's bedroom for storage. Fortunately, she was enrolled in a Munich university and wouldn't be home full time.

Amazingly, I was able to recall much of the German language I'd learned the first trip. No sooner had I landed in our stairwell apartment on post than Mike announced that he and I were going to a very formal party in just five days. I wouldn't have been concerned if the planned site was nearby, but he explained we were going to a party given by the French in a German castle several kilometers away.

On our first assignment to Fort Hood seventeen years earlier, I'd been very concerned about my being able to wear the right clothing to every occasion. Mrs. Bartlett, a slightly older wife, said, "Helen, I've learned one thing since I've been here: if you like it and it's clean and mended, wear it."

With that advice in mind, I pulled the emerald-green dress with its flowing skirt and satin sash and the open-toed black satin pumps I'd worn to Mario and Kathy's wedding from the rest of our possessions and continued to unpack boxes and put our new place in order.

The day of the ball dawned, and Cinderella Jackson had a splitting headache. No amount of begging or pleading persuaded Prince Charming Jackson to say he'd attend alone, even though we'd been told we weren't the only Americans invited to the ball.

At times such as this, any movement, light, noise, or fragrance gives me the sensation that fish hooks are being shoved up my nose to lodge in my brain. So, for this headache, I took enough over-the-counter medication to assure that I'd at least be able to endure the long ride to the castle.

On the way I reviewed what few French words I could remember from classes back in Indiana, U.S.A., and closed my eyes, hoping the medication would take effect. But, by the time we arrived at the appointed hour of five p.m., the headache had not even begun to dissipate. Before alighting from our carriage, I took some more pills and pasted my best American smile on my face. Then we stepped out of the unusually muggy summer heat into the clammy halls of the centuries-old castle.

The French military really knew how to throw a party! As guests arrived, they were treated to gifts of perfume, cigars, long-stemmed roses, and fancy souvenir programs. Festivities began, with each speechmaker decked in his best military uniform. I heard my heart beating loudly in my head. That din, combined with the difference in language, assured that I understood very little of what was said. I clapped and smiled on cue but was grateful to leave the perfume and cigars behind. The crowd dispersed into the bowels of the castle for either a ballet, stringed quintet, or jazz performance. The other guests and I then rotated among the three theaters until we'd seen each performance.

While we'd been entertained, the original gathering room was transformed into a large dining hall where the fancy program said a cold buffet would be served at ten o'clock.

After all had eaten, a young man (who'd obviously been appointed before the evening began to dance with the

American woman seated at his table) approached my chair. Gallantly bending forward ever so slightly at the waist, he held out his right arm and asked in French if I'd let him escort me to the dance floor.

With smile waning, I tried to explain that I didn't feel well-- I was dizzy. I didn't even try to communicate the fact that I wasn't a very good dancer at best. The young Frenchman wouldn't be daunted; he'd been ordered to dance with me, and dance we would!

He stepped and twirled to the orchestra music while I attempted to keep upright and in step, all the while knowing that my face was either as white as a sheet or as green as my gown.

Bless his heart, that young man made a valiant effort to smile as he brought the dizzy American back to her chair. I sat down, looking to my prince for support. I didn't think it was my imagination that led me to believe everyone else at the table, including Prince, had turned their heads to avoid laughing.

The night continued.

After what seemed hours of dancing, everyone went outside to stand and watch fireworks and a lighted, musical review featuring uniforms from different periods of French history. It was a fantastic show, but I could no longer fight the effects of too much medicine and not enough food or sleep. I allowed my practically new satin pumps to sink into the well-watered lawn, leaned upon my prince's left shoulder, and closed my eyes.

Back at post, Mike's and my work and social schedules were crammed. On the days with parades or ceremonies, I loved being a part of the old tradition. I'd heard it said in jest, "If the Army had wanted you to have a wife, they'd have issued you one." But my experience had always been that at least some measure of consideration was given to the comfort of families who lived in government quarters. During the weeks our building's bathrooms were renovated while we continued to live there, I decided the civilian decision makers honestly believed that dependents' should have been left in the States. The German workers invaded our stairwell, supposedly working on one apartment at a time. Dust billowed, and at the worst, Rick and I were forced to bathe elsewhere. It was obvious that no prior thought or concern had been given to our physical, mental, or emotional health. Mike wasn't home to listen to me whine and complain. I reasoned that if I'd been convicted of a crime and imprisoned in the United States, I'd be treated better. If I were ever tempted to lead a revolt and have my actions reflect poorly upon my husband, this was it! I escaped, instead, to the home of a friend and hid out until the mess in our apartment had cleared somewhat.

"Do not judge, and you will not be judged. Do not condemn, and you will not be condemned. Forgive, and you will be forgiven. Give, and it will be given to you. A good measure, pressed down, shaken together and running over, will be poured into your lap. For with the measure you use, it will be measured to you." Luke 6:37-38

Evidently, I wasn't the only military wife who'd taken a break from volunteering. I noticed the atmosphere surrounding volunteers seemed to have changed. It never had been a secret that Army posts, both at home and overseas, needed volunteers to function efficiently. But wives going to work outside the home had obviously diminished the total number of hours committed to volunteering. I couldn't begin to know at what level government officials decided the lack of experienced volunteers needed to be addressed. But when I received orders to go to Team Training with Mike, I knew the days of graciously following tradition were over and that fewer workers would shoulder a bigger individual workload.

Each military wife had to decide whether to work for pay, volunteer, or do her own thing. It didn't appear to be as difficult a decision for young wives as for those of us who'd volunteered in the past. I knew the unseen but long-lasting rewards of volunteering. Yet I understood many wives needed a paycheck to help finance the care for an elderly parent, pay for a college education, etc. A few wives used the term "two for one" (two workers, one government paycheck) because they felt their volunteering was expected, perhaps even demanded.

For some who couldn't decide, I shared another theory of mine: one gets back from a community in direct proportion to what she is willing to give.

Enter his gates with thanksgiving and his courts with praise; give thanks to him and praise his name. For the Lord is good and his love endures forever; his faithfulness continues through all generations. Psalm 100:4-5

Because I worked willingly (most days) around the post, the happy events of the time overseas far exceeded housing officials' overstepping the bounds of common sense and my being the worst U.S. ambassador perhaps ever to call on the French. Kathy came to visit the second summer, asking only one thing of Mike and me--that we take her to meet Mario's maternal *oma* (grandmother), who lived a few hours from our assigned workplace.

Prior to our going to Germany, Mike's grandma, Ethel Layne, of German descent, had passed away. There wasn't one of us who didn't miss her, for she was the epitome of a loving yet disciplining grandmother, *and* she made the best apple dumplings of anyone we knew. I cherished my Grandma Vermillion as well, and even though at eighty-three she was still hale and hearty when I left the States, saying good-bye to her had been tearful. I had no guarantee she'd be waiting for me when the European tour ended. The deep-seated devotion and wonderful memories associated with our grandmothers encouraged Mike and me to honor Kathy's simple yet purposeful request.

Despite the language barrier and Oma's failing health, we had a wonderful visit. No longer able to live alone or run her gasthaus (eating and drinking establishment), she pooh-poohed the notion we needed to help conserve her energy by staying only a short while. She insisted that we take pictures outside among the flowers, eat cookies, and meet as many of her own family as her granddaughter and daughter-in-law could round up. Then, after she'd been the perfect hostess, she turned to matters of the heart, asking if Mario had told Kathy of the happy times he'd shared with her when he was a little boy.

The family explained that Oma didn't always remember what she'd done the day before. I truly hoped she'd remember this day forever. What joy I received as I watched the knitting of that young American heart with the older German one. Their bonding occurred as an indirect result of Mario's and Kathy's dads willingly serving their country. How else could these two ladies have met if it hadn't been for the Plan of God, under the auspices of the U.S. Army?

Delight yourself in the Lord and he will give you the desires of your heart. Psalm 37:4

Months after Kathy's visit, while driving alone (being alone was a rare and welcomed treat) to the exchange to shop for a friend's expected-any-day baby, I became aware that this period of solitude was no accident. I realized I missed Kathy so much that if I could have willed to be with her at that moment, I would have. I didn't need her to come back to live with us; I didn't begrudge our being separated. But I did want the rest of us to return to the States as soon as possible so that we could be closer to Mario and Kathy.

Later, while shopping, my attention was distracted by a maternity outfit hanging on the sale rack. I resisted the sudden urge to buy it for Kathy and was somewhat perplexed why for a few seconds I'd even considered the purchase. On the way home, though, I thought I heard a little voice urging me to stop at the baby furniture store I'd often passed and not investigated. Leaving the shop, I said to myself, "Nothing is too good for my grandchild."

Although holding an infant in my arms hadn't stirred any desire for another baby since Rick was born, I found myself suddenly yearning to hold my grandchild.

The next morning I shared with Mary Jane Taylor, another friend who loves to laugh, that even though no one had told me I would have a grandchild soon, I was certain I was about to become a grandmother. She smiled broadly and said, "I know you want to be."

Two days later, I was awakened by an early morning trans-Atlantic telephone call.

"Mother," Kathy inquired, "Would you be happy to know your first grandchild is on the way?"

After I told Mike the good news, I hastily wrote a note and scurried to Mary Jane's front door, where I knew she'd find it when she came out for her morning newspaper. I also prayed quickly, asking the Lord to let me return to the States before my granddaughter was born.

May the God who gives endurance and encouragement give you a spirit of unity among yourselves as you follow Christ Jesus. Romans 15:5

One of the trips Mike and I took in Europe was to visit, with other American servicemen and their wives, some of World War II's battle sites. I didn't have much desire to stand on the ground where my fellow countrymen had been wounded or killed forty years or so earlier. But the only opportunity I'd have to investigate the wares of Italy, while spending time with Mike, was to tag along on the battlefield trip.

The hour spent at Sicily-Rome American Cemetery turned out to be perhaps my most outstanding memory from all the years we lived in West Germany.

Before going to the cemetery, the group stood on Anzio Beach and listened quietly as active duty men took turns explaining the significance of the terrain and the wise, and not-so-wise. decisions, made by each commander. I learned facts not taught in my history classes. I began to consider we weren't talking only about the war's statistics, but also about sons, brothers, sweethearts, and husbands.

The walk from our tour bus to the cemetery's memorial chapel took about ten minutes. Besides the footsteps of fifty-two people walking on stones, the only other sounds were the birds' voices and distant city noises, neither of which were distracting. Serenity hovered reverently over the many rows of clearly marked graves and the well-groomed grounds. I would have felt like an intruder if I hadn't sensed the presence of the Holy Spirit in this place so far removed from the nation that had sent its young to "The Big War."

As we walked down the stone path separating the nearly 8,000 gleaming white markers, I further acknowledged that each man here had given his life in the service of *my* country and was now a cherished memory to those who, willingly or unwillingly, had sent him off to serve.

Mike came to single out from the others the grave site of his uncle, Worth Jackson. I joined the rest of our group in the chapel to prepare for a memorial service as Mike visited his uncle's grave. He didn't share with me what he thought or prayed as he stood there silently.

I'm not sure what went through the minds of the military men and their wives who were on the tour with us. I suspect none of them were as overcome by emotion as I. I wept in memory of Worth, a young man only eighteen years old when he died. I cried even harder for his mother (Mike's grandmother), whose heart must have felt ripped in two when she heard the news the youngest of her four sons was missing in action. Even though Worth had been at rest for decades, her maternal wounds, I knew, were still tender. Living so far away, she would never get to stand here and grieve her loss openly.

Looking through tears over the markers, I was reminded of the day our family had visited Punch Bowl Cemetery in Hawaii. Mike's right arm, stapled and wrapped in bandages, had borne silent witness to the success of Doctor Ross's field-hospital surgery. Standing here now, in a time warp, I quietly loved my God, my husband, and our country, thanking my heavenly Father once again for sparing Mike's life during a war far less supported than his uncle's had been.

I knew the other wives couldn't understand my weeping, but I sensed a portion of my tears were for them. Their men, too, might be called to battle one day. I prayed that, if that happened, each of them--both men *and* women--would find peace. Finally, I prayed for those of our countrymen who would continue the tradition of soldiering. As I boarded the bus, I turned back to Uncle Worth's grave and those of his comrades and mouthed the words, "Thank you."

Chapter 8

Seasons of Separation

*Do not allow what you consider good to be spoken of
as evil. For the kingdom of God is not a matter of
eating and drinking, but of righteousness, peace and
joy in the Holy Spirit, because anyone who serves
Christ in this way is pleasing to God and approved
by men.* Romans 14:16-18

Mike avoided the last year of the three-year Germany
assignment by returning to the slot he'd filled prior to his
going to Europe. The job site had moved from Fort Hood to
Fort Bliss while we were in Europe. Consequently, we moved
to the part of Texas bordering New Mexico and the country of
Mexico, making me available to travel quickly when
summoned to the impending debut of Mike's and my first
grandchild.

There were no quarters for us, but I didn't care. We found
a house with the same floor plan as the one I'd loved in central
Texas. Except this one had the two improvements I'd have
made if I'd remodeled the other--another bath and doors
leading from the master bedroom to the patio. Again I knew
my heavenly Father was watching over me.

Mario had cautioned me that I was mistaken to expect a
granddaughter. I packed some tiny pink things into my
suitcase anyway. After several days of waiting, Jordan Drew,
a wonderful baby boy with brown eyes, was born. I was
definitely not disappointed to have a grandson and raved to
anyone who would listen about Mario's and Kathy's firstborn.

It wasn't until Mike declared himself too young to be called a grandfather, though, that I realized: folks who enter the military with two children may become grandparents, too, before their peers do.

I was greatly blessed to have been present when my grandson was born. But too many miles separated Jordan's and my homes, and that fact influenced my thoughts daily. Aunt Kristy, in her college apartment, lived much closer to the wonderful addition to our family than Uncle Rick, who still lived with the very young maternal grandparents.

Throughout the years, I'd intensely disliked having to say good-bye to friends I'd met at a duty station. The longer we stayed in one spot, the more good-byes. On the other hand, I loved arriving at a new post and finding a long-time friend there to greet me. Typically, I wrote enthusiastic letters to friends all over the world, attempting to keep the threads of my nomadic life tightly woven.

I was unprepared for the complications my life would encounter as my children moved, became adults, and began having children of their own. Letters were inadequate for communicating with Kathy and Kristy. None of the older military wives had told me I'd need a paycheck to finance the many calls required to stay in touch with my scattering and expanding family.

I wanted to help Mike with college bills; however, just as my daily schedule and thoughts were splintered by diversity, my energy level began to dwindle. With a grandson, a college student, a high school student, a husband who traveled, and a paying job, not to mention lugging around the extra 17 pounds I'd gained in Europe, I functioned on borderline fatigue. I made few overtures of friendship in the neighborhood, frequented the post seldom, and communicated with long-lasting friends only at Christmas time. As Jordan grew, telling him and his mommy good-bye became increasingly more difficult. I found I was happiest planning occasions when all our family (including great-grandparents) gathered to watch Jordan's newest phase. I reaped almost as much pleasure from anticipation as I did from participation in those reunions. Looking back, I see that perhaps it was a good thing I stayed busy and tired--even the best of my friends didn't understand my enthusiasm for being Jordan's grandmother.

For he will command his angels concerning you to guard you in all your ways; they will lift you up in their hands, so that you will not strike your foot against a stone. Psalm 91:11-12

We'd been blessed not to be moved as often as some other military families. When short-term assignments to Germany, West Texas, and Washington, D.C., resulted in three moves in four years, it was a new experience. In 1987, with the move to our Capital City, I counted the number of miles separating us from Jordan and didn't like the calculation.

Ordered back to Michigan after less than a year in D.C., I rejoiced I'd once again see Gus and Betty Klepper, and I hoped Mike and I could purchase another condo in their neighborhood. When we investigated the large complex, however, there wasn't a single condo on the market spacious enough for Mike, Rick, Spunky Dog, and me. We made an offer on a house across town. But the offer was not speedily submitted to the sellers, nor was it acted upon that day.

The next morning, tenants whose front door faced the Kleppers' moved out, and Betty learned the vacant condo would soon be for sale. Even though it would have to be totally renovated, it was the largest of the condo models, and I wanted to live in it.

It didn't surprise me when our offer on the house was countered and died. We quickly made an offer on the condo, shook hands with the owners to confirm our agreement, and returned to work near the seat of our national government for a few more weeks.

After we relocated, but before the massive renovations were completed, I tucked a couple of tiny pink things into my luggage and flew to Texas to help Kathy with Jordan while she neared the delivery date for Mike's and my second grandchild.

Joseph Sayre was born and disliked me immediately. I knew I was better at nurturing than predicting the sex of my grandchildren and was tempted to stay in Texas until Joseph came to his senses. But Joseph's grandpa and uncle needed me in the condo project. As I headed back to Michigan, I purposed to one day win Joseph's heart.

I'd secretly harbored thoughts before the trip that there could never be anyone else as special as Jordan. Mother and Mrs. Klepper were not surprised that, despite Joseph's attitude, he quickly found his own spot in my heart, right next to but not crowding Jordan's.

On Joseph's first Christmas, Mike, Rick, and I met our Texans at Daddy's and Mother's home in Indiana for a few days. Space was tight, and Mike and I not only were reminded of the amount of commitment and love it takes for young parents to travel with two tiny children, but also learned the grit older adults need to remain calm in the midst of the noise and clutter a young family brings. I began to better appreciate the sacrifices our parents had made to visit us wherever we moved.

Before Joseph's second Christmas, our attention turned to Desert Shield, and this time the older couples and youthful Rick traveled to Texas to celebrate.

For the eyes of the Lord range throughout the earth
to strengthen those whose hearts are fully committed
to him . . . II Chronicles 16:9a

As we and the rest of the nation gathered around television sets to observe our military preparing to do what they'd been trained to do during Desert Shield, Americans pledged support from the home front. Sensing a need to do something, many laid aside their bowling and bridge nights to support those left behind when our military forces were summoned to alert status. Americans wrote letters and sent packages by the ton to young countrymen/women serving in the desert. Many prayed around the clock. I was encouraged to see the general disenchantment of the Vietnam era replaced with pro-military sentiments.

Not every attempt to show support proved successful. Mother thoughtfully packed a box with goodies and enclosed a carefully written letter for a young man from her county she'd never met. A few weeks later, she was very disappointed to have the package return bearing the impersonal, stamped message that Andrew was an "addressee unknown."

Television reports of the buildup brought to the nation's attention the need for a strong military force at all times. The scenes coming to us via satellite reinforced the knowledge that our world communications capability had indeed changed since the time of the Vietnam conflict.

As I watched and listened to the stories of reservists being called to active duty, I thanked God my day of commitment to our country had been forced upon me years earlier. While the families of reservists scrambled to adjust their lives beyond weekend drills and summer camps, I wasn't fettered with the arduous task of preparing my heart for active duty devotion while helping my mate pack to leave home.

Finally, be strong in the Lord and in his mighty power. Ephesians 6:10

During the time of the buildup, I volunteered to ask the blessing at a luncheon for both active duty and retired military wives at the nearby base.

When I sat down to collect my thoughts, I knew the presence of the Lord was in the room with me, inspiring me to write.

Dear Lord,

We gather today not only for lunch and fellowship, but also to seek solace in the togetherness of generations of women who support their military men. We are thankful You've turned the heart of our nation to openly showing support for American military men and women. We are grateful You are there with them and You continue to watch over their equipment and water.

Your word says You are the same yesterday, today, and forever. So we ask as in the days of Joshua, the enemy's walls come tumbling down; as in the days of David, our sophisticated stones hit their intended and targeted equipment. As in the days of Daniel, Shadrach, Meshach, and Abednego, You deliver our troops out of enemy's devices and protect each and every one; and as in the days of Paul, the doors which restrain American Prisoners Of War fling open to free them.

In obedience to your word, I ask You to be merciful even to Sadaam Hussain.

And then, Lord we do ask You to bless this food to strengthen our mortal bodies. We ask all this in Your mighty name. Amen.

He makes wars cease to the ends of the earth; he breaks the bow and shatters the spear, he burns the shields with fire. "Be still and know that I am God; I will be exalted among the nations, I will be exalted in the earth." Psalm 46:9-10

While planes and artillery flew, tanks rumbled, and television stations kept us abreast of the war's events, I kept myself isolated in the condo's basement. Several times a day I prayed for our President and others in leadership and then for the lengthening list of men and women I knew personally who were on the ground or had been called from reserve status to active duty. Then I prayed for the families left behind. Those men, women, boys, and girls needed my heavenly Father to take away the knots in their stomachs, the tears from their eyes, and the nagging fear so they, too, would be able to pray with faith.

To keep my hands busy, I cross-stitched most of two pillow tops. I didn't cook; I didn't clean house. The Holy Spirit had permission to draw strength from me and take it to my countrymen and women.

My husband hadn't been pulled to the Middle East for combat, but his nephew Michael Anthony Jackson, a Marine, had been. Armed with the knowledge our God had been faithful, was faithful, and always would be faithful, I enclosed prayers with Michael's home-baked cookies. As with other benefits of being God's child, those prayers didn't take up any space in the box nor require added postage!

Our family breathed a collective sigh of relief when we learned Michael, our friends, and almost all of our other troops would return safely. There is no doubt in my mind prayers of Americans were answered. It takes nothing away from personnel, plans, operations, equipment, or our reputation as peacekeepers to say God answered our prayers.

Chapter 9

There Is a Time

All you have made will praise you, O Lord; your saints will extol you. They will tell of the glory of your kingdom and speak of your might, so that all men may know of your mighty acts and the glorious splendor of your kingdom. Your kingdom is an everlasting kingdom, and your dominion endures through all generations. The Lord is faithful to all his promises and loving toward all he has made.
Psalm 145:10-13

Military wives, whether they love the life, hate it, or stand somewhere on middle ground, know that after the seasons of separations, schools, and intensive training with units have cycled, retirement will come. The *unknowns* make each wonder if she'll be prepared and able to adjust.

I knew that when Mike and I retired from active duty, I wanted to be near Kathy's family and Kristy, who'd graduated from college in Texas and stayed. Part of me, however, felt guilty for wanting to move back to central Texas to be near the younger generations while Mike's mother, Margaret, and my parents remained in Indiana.

Just as Margaret had waited for her brother, Bill Layne, to return from Europe after World War II; just as she'd prayed for her sons, Ron, Mike, and Tony, to return from Vietnam; she wore a yellow ribbon fastened to her coat lapel to show support for her country and her belief that her grandson Michael and his generation would come home safely from overseas. However, Michael had not returned to the States when Margaret suddenly passed away in March, 1991.

Margaret and I had become solid friends while she lived with us in Texas, and she and Mother cemented their friendship when she left our home and returned to live in Indiana. Neither Mother nor I was prepared for just how much we'd grieve. Mother repeatedly expressed the sentiment she *missed* her friend, my mother-in-law.

During my visit to Indiana six months after Margaret's funeral, Mother again sighed and said, "I still miss Margaret so much."

Mother's transparency gave me reason to reflect. On the drive back to Michigan, I began to rethink my desire to move to Texas when Mike retired. Although the process of daily living went on without Margaret, I began to sense everything in my life had changed. The questions came: Should we move to Texas? Should we move to Indiana, at least temporarily? Should we stay in Michigan? Should I promise to visit my parents every three or four months after we'd moved to Texas? Could I get my folks to follow us to Texas once we'd settled there?

Trust in the Lord with all your heart and lean not on your own understanding; in all your ways acknowledge him, and he will make your paths straight. Proverbs 3:5-6

Only nine days lapsed between Mother's telling me she continued to miss Margaret and my attending the funeral of a dear old saint of my Michigan church. During the service, I was certain I heard a whisper in my left ear, "You'll walk through this valley very soon." I didn't want to listen, nor could I tell my best buddy, Rita DeArmond, who sat beside me, why I was so broken.

Back in the security of our home, I cried out to God, "I don't want to hear it. I don't want to hear it."

Nevertheless, I was forced to listen. Three days and nine hours later, my mother literally stepped out of this life and into the next.

When my friend Jesus left this earth, He said he would send a comforter for His followers. He, the Holy Spirit, came immediately to wrap me in His invisible arms and to assure my heart that it was Mother's time to be with our heavenly Father. I knew instantly she no longer missed Margaret's fellowship.

You are the salt of the earth. . . You are the light of the world. . . Let your light shine before men, that they may see your good deeds and praise your Father in heaven. Matthew 5:13a;14a;16b

Mother hadn't told me, but I knew she had been discouraged when her package didn't reach Andrew and probably felt as if she hadn't done anything else of great importance for her country. I knew better. She'd staunchly supported me in my role, praying as if she'd chosen for me to leave the area where she and Daddy had devotedly reared me. Rising above the disappointment of our being geographically removed from her, she'd constantly praised the Lord for inspiring mankind to invent the telephone, automobile, and airplane. Those technical inventions, as well as audio tapes and movie cameras, had knit her life with those of her family while she stayed home and prayed.

Mother had denied herself a few creature comforts to travel to see her grandchildren. She had much to share with them, and she was determined to do it. She needed no formal instruction to pray for her grandchildren every day. As adults, my kids were sometimes embarrassed when she pulled them onto her lap and expressed her love for them as she'd done when they were small, but there was never a doubt in their minds that she loved them greatly and wanted them to become all God wanted them to be.

She wanted world peace and for there to be no need for our country to have a strong fighting force. But she'd read her Bible and was realistic. She knew that there would always be rumors of war and a need for national defense. More than the desire for wars to cease, she wanted people she'd met to make their peace with God. She'd been a lighthouse, as evidenced by the many who told me how she'd touched their lives both in big and small ways.

At a point in my life when everything in my being wanted to know if the pain of losing Mother and Margaret would ever ease, I acknowledged that I must pick up the responsibilities of their generation, and once again forge ahead into change.

Oddly enough, it was my daddy's 90-year-old mother, Grandma Vermillion, who gave me courage. I looked into her tired eyes and saw that she'd been a good mother, grandmother, and great-grandmother despite the fact she hadn't had a happy childhood. There had been no personal rewards for serving as a military wife at the end of World War I, yet she didn't let that keep her from praying for me daily while I was away. She'd buried three husbands before her sixty-fifth birthday, but I never once heard her, when she was lonely, accuse God of being unfair. Her brood of three sons, seven grandchildren, twelve great-grandchildren, and two great-great-grandchildren (Jordan and Joseph) were much too busy, she'd declared repeatedly. Nevertheless, when one of us stopped by her home to visit or called her on the telephone, her voice strengthened, and she faithfully recounted the week's visitors and expressed quite clearly her opinions of the

world's current events as they related to her and her Bible.
She'd never shunned hard work and expected us to do our
best. She also expected each of us to do things God's way.
When we felt we'd failed, she was faithful to help lead us back
to the place where we could expect a brighter tomorrow,
reminding us that her family was the best in the nation. She
repeatedly stated that my Grandpa Homer would have been
very proud of a family that "didn't have a bad one among
'em."

Yes, going on would be difficult, but Grandma, all four-
and-a-half feet of her, knew the way. I vowed to embrace my
rich heritage and follow Grandma's example.

*There is a time for everything, and a season for
every activity under heaven: . . . A time to weep and
a time to laugh, a time to mourn and a time to
dance.* Ecclesiastes 3:1,4

Mother had loved to tell stories, and she'd told most of her
friends how Kristy, a senior at Ellison High, met Michael
Adame, graduate of rival Killeen High.

"It all began," she'd say, "right after Helen's husband,
Mike, went to Europe the last time. I believe it was by Divine
guidance Michael and Kristy met the first weekend of
February, 1984. I'm not sure who was following whom that
particular weekend, but each attended a Friday night
basketball game and a Saturday night dance before Michael's
nephew David introduced them to each other at church
Sunday evening.

"When Michael came to take Kristy for a drive shortly after
they met, Kristy wasn't quite ready, so Rick invited Michael to
sit and wait in the den. Kristy came out just in time to hear

Rick tell Michael that he, Rick, wanted him, Michael, to be his next brother-in-law.

"I suspect," Mother would smile, "that Kristy didn't know whether to make her appearance or duck back into her bedroom. I do know she was embarrassed. She'd told me at the time that she believed this young man was very, very special. Helen agreed. Kristy's daddy, grandpa, and I didn't get to meet Michael until the Army took the Jacksons to El Paso in 1986. While Harold and I visited, Michael came for a couple of days just before he left Texas for basic training in South Carolina. *I* liked him from the start.

"It's been both fascinating and bewildering to watch this courtship. Here it is, seven-and-a-half years later, and they are finally going to get married."

Mother, who adored her grandchildren, had readily accepted Mario as her grandson-in-love, and had purchased her airplane ticket to Texas well in advance of the wedding date Michael and Kristy had set. She'd stated she hated to sew anymore, but she began making a quilt for the couple and gave Kristy unsolicited but welcome marriage advice.

Less than three weeks after Mother's funeral, Michael and Kristy married in Texas. All of us knew my mother would have wanted us to proceed on down life's pathway as planned.

I'm sure Mike Jackson was just as handsome as he'd been when he walked Kathy down the aisle. I have photos to prove Kristy was as beautiful in her wedding gown as Kathy had been in hers. But I don't remember watching my husband make that walk with our younger daughter. My physical energy had been drained; my mind was somewhat detached. Yet, my wonderful heavenly Father had sent friends, both military and civilian, to support me, and I was overwhelmingly aware my emotions were cradled in the hands of the Holy Spirit comforter.

Even youths grow tired and weary, and young men stumble and fall; but those who hope in the Lord will renew their strength. They will soar on wings like eagles; they will run and not grow weary, they will walk and not be faint. Isaiah 40:30-31

Although I'd said I wouldn't encourage Mike to retire before he was ready, he traveled constantly and lost so much sleep that I had difficulty keeping my mouth shut. The bags under his eyes made it appear as if his eyes were sinking into his head. The weekends he shared with Rick and me were, in reality, times of recuperating from his national and international travels.

I asked myself if Mike would hang up his spurs before he was totally spent. Meanwhile, I clung to one last dream--that of having a youthful husband with whom to share retirement. I suggested he needed a vacation, but there was no time in Mike's projected schedule for even a short one. Nevertheless, after he'd reconsidered his priorities, we went to Hawaii for nearly a week, just the two of us this time, to celebrate our upcoming thirtieth wedding anniversary. By the end of the trip, the bags under Mike's eyes had vanished, his beautiful blue eyes sparkled, his sun-kissed cheeks glowed, and his frown lines were diminished.

As our plane landed in Detroit, I thanked my heavenly Father again for His statement and affirmation that it wasn't good for Mike to live alone (Genesis 2:18).

My dream revived.

"...This day is sacred to our Lord. Do not grieve, for the joy of the Lord is your strength." Nehemiah 8:10b

Even if one in the U. S. Army were convinced he were ready to retire (and I knew Mike wasn't), there might not be a convenient time when all one wanted to accomplish was completed. Whether issuing new equipment, planning upcoming field training, preparing for the motor pool inspection, changing personnel in the office, or renovating the dining facility (new name for the mess hall), there would always be one more hurdle for the devoted, to make retiring look as if it should be postponed.

Knowing that Mike's wrestling with the decision of whether to retire or not was dramatically more difficult than the one I'd already made in its favor, I began to pray God would give my husband supernatural strength until the day he decided to submit his retirement papers. Within me, there was a struggle, too. One second I wanted to stay near Betty and my pals as long as the Army would let me; the next I wanted to race to Texas.

My heart was pulled to my wonderful and hurting daddy. Both he and Mother had told me before Mother died that Daddy wouldn't last long if anything happened to Mother. She'd said Daddy needed to remarry quickly and instructed me not to get in his way. As unselfish as her wishes for Daddy appeared, Mother, I thought, left me with the overwhelming responsibility to see that Daddy remarried. I'd had only three days' notice that someone I loved was heaven-bound, and I certainly wasn't ready to lose him.

When I wasn't visiting with Betty Klepper or Rita DeArmond or thinking about moving to be closer to Jordan and Joseph, I'd wrack my brain to think of just the right woman to line up for my precious dad, forgetting it was my privilege to love Daddy through his time of grief and allow God to heal and then reveal His plan for Daddy's future.

In a matter of weeks, Mike began to talk of retiring and preparing to make plans to send me to an area not far from Fort Hood to select a building site for a home in which we would retire. Many questions and ideas whirled in my head. It was difficult to concentrate. Finally, in 1992, Mike gave me the okay to seriously and openly make retirement plans. Change was on its way, and this time, I welcomed it wholeheartedly.

Blessed is the man who perseveres under trial, because when he has stood the test, he will receive the crown of life that God has promised to those who love him. James 1:12

Still not liking most other changes, I planned fewer of them once Mike retired and we'd settled in Texas. Amid the pulling back from my Michigan friends (knowing I would leave them soon) and the excitement of moving closer to my daughters and their families, Rick made plans to leave home. After he'd earned his associate's degree in Michigan and helped us settle into the new house in Texas, he'd go.

I'd given the term "empty nest" and its implication very little thought, even though I'd known mothers who described their last child's departure as nothing short of traumatic. Listening to them, I discerned their separations had been as catastrophic as if their children had been marooned on an island. Even if the mother had nudged or shoved her child out, she no longer felt as needed as when her children were younger. To varying degrees, those mothers seemed to sense a desire to return to the security of days gone by, days of snuggling, lullaby singing, and knowing her last child was "safe."

I wanted to approach my empty nest logically. At the time of Rick's contemplated leaving, he'd be older than I'd been when Mike and I married, and the results of my efforts to prepare Rick for becoming a bachelor far exceeded my expectations. He'd developed principles of fairness, generosity, tenderness, and compassion I had previously thought foreign to young men. Yet he was tough and tenacious, weighing his capabilities and limitations with much thought and accuracy. He was prepared for change.

Let us then approach the throne of grace with confidence, so that we may receive mercy and find grace to help us in our time of need. Hebrews 4:16

To look into my only son's blue eyes, I had to stand on the step above him. The twinkle that I'd come to know as his acknowledging our mutual love and appreciation made me want to shout, "Hey, world, this is my kid."

We both knew the rules. He did all the talking. With his hands on my shoulders, he'd ask, "Have I told my mommy that I love her yet today?" He knew that he hadn't. Depending upon what he'd read in *my* eyes, he followed his question with either a very gentle or a very loud kiss on my cheek.

I would miss his humor and his big bear hugs. Despite my desire to be logical, I fought anxiety daily and dreaded the thought of his leaving. I was forced to ask myself if I were troubled at the prospect of being lonely or the stigma others attached to the empty nest.

Even though children were supposed to grow in confidence and leave home, bringing about change, I wasn't sure this final step into Rick's being on his own could be considered progress. Whatever the cause of my distress, I purposed not to allow my sense of loss to overtake joy, creating the perception Rick's impending move would overwhelm or devastate me. I knew there might be internal wounding on the inevitable day of Rick's leaving, but, at all cost, I didn't want him to see the pain nipping at my heart. Expectancy and loss played teeter-

totter there with such gusto, I didn't know whether to laugh
or cry. Instead, I wrote:

Dear Lord,
   Help me to be sensitive to the needs of my only son
when he is away. Awaken me in the night to pray
when he is discouraged. Quicken my spirit when he is
in danger. Remind him You never leave him nor
forsake him. I love You, Father. I thank You for Rick
and the cherished memories no one can take from me.
I now release him to You, to let him fly from his
father's and my nest. Empty? No. Lonely? Perhaps.
Grateful? Definitely. Thanks! Helen

*Though he stumble, he will not fall, for the Lord
upholds him with his hand. I was young and now I
am old, yet I have never seen the righteous forsaken
or their children begging bread. They are always
generous and lend freely; their children will be
blessed.* Psalm 37:24-26

   I thought I would be able to let go of Rick and believe for
his peaceful existence apart from Mike's and my home. For
me, leaving Indiana had brought fear and caused me to focus
inward. But having survived the trek of life to the brink of
retirement, and now being a part of the *older* generation, it
would be tempting to sit around and talk about the "good old
days" rather than to assess changes and continue to march.
   During Mike's active duty, we'd seen our country begin to
spend more money taking care of young soldiers and their
families. We'd watched the strategy change from preparing to
fight World War II, Korea, and Vietnam all over again to
training various specialty units who could be deployed

quickly. Our country moved from all-out efforts to fight communism to looking for unpredictable tyrants who want to make their point by being nasty. The Berlin Wall had come down, but we now received threats from organizations which years ago were merely annoyances. The world had, indeed, changed.

At some point in the near future, Mike and I would ease out of the way and allow the younger ones to do things their way. Yet, I trusted we'd continue to remain active, preventing stagnation.

Heaven and earth will pass away, but my words will never pass away. Matthew 24:35

Rick looked forward to the adventures the world held for him. I hoped he was unaware the older, more experienced part of me cringed when I looked at current national policies and the world chaos which waited for his generation to conquer.

That knowledge, coupled with my experiences, led me to believe lives of servicemen/women entering the military as Mike left would have more pressures than we'd had. The cares of our world aren't any less burdensome for those outside the military. Yet, I'm encouraged to find faith rising in me for young adults who want and are prepared to leave home. Where is the encouragement coming from, if not from the One Who never changes but Who'd guided me through all the changes of Mike's active duty days?

So then, those who suffer according to God's will should commit themselves to their faithful Creator and continue to do good. I Peter 4:19

I rejoice that, even though more and more military spouses find they must work outside the home and other external influences often crowd out family time, I have overwhelming confidence that those families, like ours, will be able to stick together no matter what. Joy springs in my heart to know there are generations of women to come who, despite changing community requirements, will remain committed to their husbands and our God. It is not that I have any more faith in my kids' generation. Rather, it is my faith in our God.

Since, then, you have been raised with Christ, set your hearts on things above, where Christ is seated at the right hand of God. Set your minds on things above, not on earthly things. Colossians 3:1-2

There are those who wring their hands over the state of our global economy, pollution, and the perception that our American military commitments are too far-reaching. I am confident some are looking for solutions in the wrong places, buying into the false theory that people must "find themselves" rather than the truth that they must *find God*.

I am still confident of this: I will see the goodness of the Lord in the land of the living. Wait for the Lord; be strong and take heart and wait for the Lord. Psalm 27:13-14

Yes, the country is in a mess! Yet, I've witnessed God inspire and prod humans to become solution-minded. I'm confident that He, the One Who created the Universe and who numbered the hairs of our heads and who cares about every sparrow who falls to the ground (Matthew 10:29-30), knew this day of personal and national poor choices would come. The Lord already knows to whom He will entrust the answers for current and future problems.

If my people who are called by my name, will humble themselves and pray and seek my face and turn from their wicked ways, then will I hear from heaven and will forgive their sin and will heal their land. II Chronicles 7:14

The solutions won't come in the wringing of hands, worrying, picketing, name-calling, or looking for someone else to blame. No, the answers will come from each one of us (not just chaplains and other clergy) praying and then doing his or her part to preserve and protect what is good and stand firm against evil.

Some might say I'm looking through rose-colored glasses. But I love God's promises, which tell us that if we do *this*, then our heavenly Father will do *that*. It's a pretty awesome thought: praying people who turn from wicked ways and turn to God will see their land healed. I choose to believe Him, and I'm confident someone who prays will be called to unearth the much needed solutions. Perhaps he or she will come from a military family. After all, they're known to be resourceful, assess change accurately, bloom where they're planted, and lend a helping hand wherever and whenever it is needed.

Chapter 10

With All Your Might

*By faith Abraham, when called to go to a place he
would later receive as his inheritance, obeyed and
went, even though he did not know where he was
going. By faith he made his home in the promised
land like a stranger in a foreign country.* Hebrews
11:8-9a

There were days I thought I knew how Abraham felt! But
throughout history God has sent people to places unknown to
do the things He asked, blessing their obedient efforts. He
chose some to serve their nations and anointed them for war.
He recorded the stories of David and Joshua in the Bible so
folks like me who'd never known much about serving their
country would be assured that moving about with the military
is an honorable thing to do.

Everywhere we went, Mike and I were told, "This is not
the real Army." The real Army, some said, wasn't the Vietnam
buildup or a tour there. Others argued that it wasn't schools
or guarding the East/West German border, nor was it in the
Pentagon, sleeping on the hood of a jeep, or on a rifle range.
As a matter of fact, no one ever told me what constitutes the
real Army. I had to draw my own conclusions: the real Army
is dedicated, self-sacrificing folks called from all parts of the
country and trained for war. They train with all their might
and then leave with very little notice for places their
countrymen probably wouldn't want to go. Most, I think,
hope and pray that they never have to pull a trigger for

anything other than training, always concerned for those who
must live with the consequences of their decisions. They
believe their nation is the best and are willing and ready to
fight for her dignity and honor. Real Army folks are loved and
cherished not only by the family into which they were born,
adopted, or married but also by a whole host of other
wonderful people known as the military community.

Teamwork is built not only through training but also
through acknowledging that each man needs the other. The
real Army knows the spotlight can't be on everyone all the
time. Various specialties within the Army may claim that
they're better than the unit down the street, but when the truth
is told, they celebrate finely tuned teamwork and deeply
appreciate the talent and dedication the other units offer the
country.

*Whatever your hand finds to do, do it with all your
might* . . . Ecclesiastes 9:10a

Mike, like others on the Army team, did what he was called
to do. While his duties and responsibilities (and even our
enemies) changed throughout the years, he remained true to
his calling. Seldom did he question whether the family's
sacrifice of time without him was avoidable. He was focused
and devoted. His medals and stacks of certificates verify he
did a good job. He'd leave active duty with fulfillment (an
award we can't hang on his office wall) and friends who will
be loyal to their last breath.

The closer time for retiring came, I watched Mike as he
struggled with leaving the Army and as he watched me
agonize over my upcoming empty nest. One day the transition
sounded liberating; the next, the idea weighed down his
countenance.

There was one thread of my life's tapestry which needed to be neatly knotted and put away. For twenty years, I'd wanted to thank Doctor Ross for being where he was called and doing his job expertly. Oh, I knew I could have written him a letter, but my heart's desire was to look him in the eye and express my gratitude.

Although I didn't know it when it happened, Doctor Ross had wanted to send my wounded husband from Vietnam to Japan, where doctors he considered experts could work on Mike's arm. Nevertheless, with the One to Whom I prayed looking over his shoulder, the doc had done the impossible--he put Mike's right arm back together so that it functioned as before.

More than twenty-three years later, the super soldiers who served with Mike and Doctor Ross held a reunion in Huntsville, Alabama. There, in a hotel dining room at a time in my life when multiple changes surrounded all facets of my life, I thanked Doctor Ross. He told me he was pleased he'd been there to help. No parade, flares, or trumpets to mark this occasion--just the expression and acceptance of the long-nurtured gratitude, the opportunity to tie up loose ends before packing the household goods and heading to Texas.

Doctor Ross had left the Army after the Vietnam conflict and gone into private practice. Between that time and the time Mike planned to leave active duty, nearly every other member of their unit had hung up his uniform and scattered among the civilians.

Mike, too, would soon take off the uniform. Both of us knew that no matter what kind of civilian clothing he wore, his heart would remain with the young soldier. He wanted the young to have the best training and equipment our country could realistically afford. As he prepared to pass the baton to them, he would rest in the knowledge that his generation's dedication is mirrored by each generation on the team.

For God was pleased to have all his fullness dwell in
him, and through him to reconcile to himself all
things, whether things on earth or things in heaven,
by making peace through his blood, shed on the
cross. Colossians 1:19-20

As I reflected upon the past twenty-five years, I realized I
hadn't just tagged along behind Mike, who dealt with young
men and their tanks, fuel, budgets, plans, and safety
procedures. Rather, I was called to his side to daily mesh
God-fearing motherhood with the lives of other women and
children so that our family's devotion to America would be
balanced. Each of us was called to serve our country and its
people--Mike in the Army, and I as his dependable dependent.

God blessed our efforts of service. He was faithful to
weave military tradition with civilian roots, security of
farmlands with the adventure of travel, my dreams with His
Plan. He was also faithful to show me that my United States
military photo I.D. hadn't taken away my individuality, but
rather authenticated my spot in our worldwide community. I'd
changed; I'd grown.

Keep on loving each other as brothers. Do not forget
to entertain strangers, for by so doing some people
have entertained angels without knowing it. Hebrews
13:1-2

At some point, the Army changed my designation from
"dependent" to "family member." By the time they did it, it
didn't matter to me anymore. It wasn't the title or my
immature reaction to the term, but the relationships Army
living brought into my life which were important. As

embarrassing as it is to admit, the paths I dreaded traveling unearthed the most wisdom, and the places I least wanted to go produced the best friends.

Most of the God-given treasures I carry from active duty days are those relationships. He put many a Jewel (although they answer to other first names) in my path that I might rejoice in the way He laid out for me. He has my gratitude for orchestrating loving and gifted folks into my life.

After Job had prayed for his friends, the Lord made him prosperous once again and gave him twice as much as he had before. Job 42:10

Some moves were easier than others, but I shudder to think what would have happened if I hadn't been shoved from my central Indiana nest and exposed to the wonderful folks who make up the Army family. The rewards of God's plan to have our paths cross keep rolling in. Many of my friends are now grandmothers who storm heaven when another's grandchild needs Divine intervention. There is great comfort in knowing those prayer warriors are only a telephone call away.

Praying and seeing the answers changes one's attitudes in every season of coming, staying, and going. As military spouses, Linda and I learned to depend upon each other in both the happy and sad times. Within military communities, reaching out to a friend or a newly arrived stranger is still an accepted custom.

Good-bye to my hats, gloves, calling cards, and mess halls; I'm grateful the dread, fear, and dismal attitudes of 1967 are buried, as well. Welcome computers and those who believe with me that God is awesome.

Like Linda, I truly appreciate the Lord's allowing me to pray for couples who want babies. On many occasions, as I reached out in love to them, the Lord heard our unified cry and gave them the desires of their hearts. His nature is to turn bad situations into good. He has truly worked miracles, opening wombs and oiling the hinges of adoption procedures. I would love to magnify His Name by writing about His answers to those prayers. But those are the tender stories of His magnificent greatness deposited in the hearts of other mothers. If those babies or their parents pass through central Texas, I will want them to know that my antique rocking chair and a glass of iced tea or mug of hot chocolate waits for them!

We love because he first loved us. I John 4:19

Not when it happened, but now, I treasure Mike's determination not to bend to family and community pressure to stay in a job not made for him, but to pursue the one that was. Most of all, I cherish his and my children's friendships. Only now that we're all adults do I understand our being friends enabled us to accept and conquer individual inconveniences brought about by Army orders. I'm happy to say that God certainly knew what He was doing when He put us in the Army community.

Do not conform any longer to the pattern of this world, but be transformed by the renewing of your mind. Then you will be able to test and approve what God's will is--his good, pleasing and perfect will.
Romans 12:2

I'm grateful that I couldn't change the will of God with all of my questions, but through my questioning, He was able to change my mind. I was ready to quit moving about, but I wanted to continue encouraging others to flexibly follow their husbands and joyfully listen for the voice of God.

What had I learned? What could I share with those following that would make their paths easier?

Is any one of you in trouble? He should pray. Is anyone happy? Let him sing songs of praise. Is any one of you sick? He should call the elders of the church to pray over him and anoint him with oil in the name of the Lord. And the prayer offered in faith will make the sick person well; the Lord will raise him up. If he has sinned, he will be forgiven. Therefore confess your sins to each other and pray for each other so that you may be healed. The prayer of a righteous man is powerful and effective. Elijah was a man just like us. He prayed earnestly that it would not rain, and it did not rain on the land for three and a half years. Again he prayed, and the heavens gave rain, and the earth produced its corps.
James 5:13-18

If one were to ask any of my friends if she wishes she'd been allowed to walk my path, I'm confident her answer would be a resounding no. Is there any one else's path I wish had been mine? No. But time has proven our meeting and praying together increased our faith and made a difference in the confidence with which we walked our individual paths once we were separated.

God laid out those plans, and along my path He allowed me to make choices. I left Indiana the first time figuratively kicking, screaming, and dragging my heels. Yet, I'm glad I made that choice. I suspect I'd have been miserable staying where I thought I was secure because there is no security outside God's plan for me.

Your word is a lamp to my feet and a light for my path. Psalm 119:105

Did I like leaving my family and friends in Indiana? No, but it got easier with time. I realized for whatever reason, God allowed them to stay, but He'd called me elsewhere. As I read that He'd said, "I will never leave you," I inserted my name. It gave me courage to read with my heart, "I will never leave you, Helen."

Did I like leaving my military sisters time after time? No, but the friendships weren't terminated because we separated. God said that the end is better than the beginning, and I gained hope.

Was it fun to live through the Vietnam era? No, but I became more reliant on God. Jesus said, "I am the way, the truth, and the life." Reading those words, I learned to place greater trust in the God of my childhood.

Am I glad Rick's leg fractured four times? No, but I'm definitely grateful my son was born the minute God ordained and he's not crippled. My God said to be strong and courageous, and He gave me increased faith in His strength.

Do I have regrets? Sure, but those regrets come from the realization I made poor choices, not that God ever left me or that He didn't design the best plan for me. He said to choose whom I would serve. He knew my struggling through making choices would make me flexible.

Did I like seeing my earthly possessions dented, rubbed, scratched, and marred? No, but *I'm* stronger. My heavenly Father said that even when I walk through the valley of the shadow of death, I don't have to fear any evil because He's with me. He promised to guide me with His rod and staff. He, my awesome God, promised to spread a table out in front of me in the presence of my enemies; Jesus promised to send a comforter, and I was comforted.

There were times I felt myself a victim of the system which took me half way around the world twice, but He said that He would not let my foot slip. In reflection, I realized God Himself gave me an opportunity I would never have had any other way. The folks in Washington, D.C., when issuing Mike's orders, looked primarily at the needs of the military. But God planned each and every assignment for Helen, Kathy, Kristy, and Rick with their needs in mind.

Through it all, my questioning never changed what God *said* about me, His child.

(For scriptures referenced, see Hebrews 13:5b; John 14:6; Ecclesiastes 7:8; Joshua 1:6; Joshua 24:15; Psalm 23:4-5; John 14:16; and Psalm 121:3).

It is for freedom that Christ has set us free. Stand firm, then, and do not let yourselves be burdened again by a yoke of slavery. Galatians 5:1

It was by God's mercy I was born in the United States of America, reared on a central Indiana farm, and married Michael D. Jackson. I'd been in training wherever Uncle Sam sent Mike. I'm confident there were times I lacked wisdom, and even though Mike told me to be myself, he wished I'd imitate others who weren't as independent. Sometimes I wanted to ignore the Army way, God's way, and/or Mike's way to do things *my* way. Nearly every regret I have, though, took root in periods of rebellion. After several of those unprofitable times, I learned God was directing me to conform to His Way and, thereby, to change. He, more than Mike, wanted me to become and perfect who He called me to be.

Reflecting upon the sin of murmuring, I've had to repent the number of times over the years I resented God's taking me away from the farmlands and my dreams. Facing Mike's retirement, I had to admit I was glad God, and to a lesser degree, Mike, knew better than I, in 1967, where we were going and what we should learn.

As a result of Mike's and my being closer to our children and grandchildren in the '90s, there would be welcome demands upon my time, but I anticipated being able to put down my own roots, both figuratively and literally, to plant bulbs and trees in our yard and watch them grow to maturity.

Once I began to grasp the idea that my adventure is planned by the Heavenly Commander, I was more eager to get on with it. I was forced to take inventory of my attitudes and evaluate what I wanted to be "when I grew up." Oh, yes, I wanted to go to Texas, but more than that, I wanted to know what God had waiting for me there. I had to assume my new experiences would be an extension of the old, perfectly suited to *my* energy, time, temperament, interests, and location! With a stationary command post and new missions, retirement could be interesting. I must keep listening to my Heavenly Father-Commander, rejoicing that He would keep spit-shining me.

> *Do not store up for yourselves treasures on earth, where moth and rust destroy, and where thieves break in and steal. But store up for yourselves treasures in heaven, where moth and rust do not destroy, and where thieves do not break in and steal. For where your treasure is, there your heart will be also.* Matthew 6:19-20

No matter the year on my calendar or my age, I see that childlike faith continues to touch the throne of God. From the high chair to the rocking chair, His way is best for me, and I love the prospect of His retirement plan. One day He'll allow me to leave the bugles of training and listen for the sound of harps. The ceremony will be called a funeral. Only in that retirement home called heaven will I encounter no more suspicious refrigerator repairmen, tearful farewells, or change.

> . . . *Christ Jesus, who died--more than that, who was raised to life--is at the right hand of God and is also interceding for us. Who shall separate us from the love of Christ? Shall trouble or hardship or persecution or famine or nakedness or danger or sword? As it is written: "For your sake we face death all day long; we are considered as sheep to be slaughtered." No, in all these things we are more than conquerors through him who loved us. For I am convinced that neither death nor life, neither angels nor demons, neither the present nor the future, nor any powers, neither height nor depth, nor anything else in all creation, will be able to separate us from the love of God that is in Christ Jesus our Lord.*
> Romans 8:34b-39

I've asked my heavenly Father and my earthly daddy, and I've been asked by others, why God allows devastating things to happen in our lives. I still don't have an answer.

I do know, as I learn of God's character, that He is compassionate. He isn't, as some would paint Him, always angry, poised to thump a hurting child on the head with an oversized gavel. He sent His Son, Jesus, to show us, by example, how to live with the good and the bad. When Jesus lived here, faithful prayer preceded His taking action. When Satan tried to tempt Him, He quoted what God had said.

When He was in a tight spot, He preferred His Father's will to His own. Now, as then, God sends rain on the righteous and unrighteous (Matthew 5:45), but painful things in a life hurt far worse than sprinkles, gully-washers, or anything in between. The pain sometimes causes us to question if we are the righteous or unrighteous.

One doesn't have to experience each and every trial known to mankind to understand that any one trial when it involves *her* family, can wound, fracture, or paralyze. She can hurt so badly that she doesn't know where to turn. The one trap she mustn't fall into is to blame God. James 1:13-18 explains that God does not tempt anyone with evil and cannot be tempted by evil. The passage reminds us that every good and perfect gift is from above.

I have to believe, after all the years lived and miles traveled, that some woes come as a result of one or more poor choices and many our Lord allows so we can learn to depend entirely upon Him.

Brothers, as an example of patience in the face of suffering, take the prophets who spoke in the name of the Lord. As you know, we consider blessed those who have persevered. You have heard of Job's perseverance and have seen what the Lord finally brought about. The Lord is full of compassion and mercy. James 5:10-11

Throughout the Bible, He had men of old record His desire for a loving relationship with man. It is through that relationship one learns who He is and His characteristics. Since he already knows all there is to know about us, the purpose of the relationship must be then that He wants us to know Him.

If I could leave the military community with one piece of advice for facing hardship, it would be: let God, full of compassion and mercy, kindle a loving relationship with you before the hardships come.

> *"Come to me, all you who are weary and burdened, and I will give you rest. Take my yoke upon you and learn from me, for I am gentle and humble in heart, and you will find rest for your souls. For my yoke is easy and my burden is light."* Matthew 11:28-30

Something in our nature tends to credit God with things not His doing. We say we've had "good luck" when we approve of what has happened, yet call a disaster an "act of God." Even if we misunderstand where our troubles originate, we still have a choice either to allow Christ Jesus to make the way easier or to try to work through it alone.

Many folks do, it seems, tend to turn to God more in the bad times than in the good. During Desert Storm, for instance, some folks prayed then who hadn't prayed in years. Why?

It's sad to say, but when God answered those prayers, some moseyed off to do their own thing until another crisis presented itself. God's kind and gentle promise was ignored.

> *Find rest, O my soul, in God alone; my hope comes from him. He alone is my rock and my salvation; he is my fortress, I will not be shaken. My salvation and my honor depend on God; he is my mighty rock, my refuge. Trust in him at all times, O people; pour out your hearts to him, for God is our refuge.*
> Psalm 62:5-8

Isn't this another perfect prayer for a military wife?
Although the U.S. government tries, it just can't cover all
what ifs in our lives. God can. In her class on prayer, Mary
Jane Taylor teaches that one doesn't have to be able to pray
with great words and long sentences to communicate with
God. One only has to be able to utter the short but effective
prayer: "Lord?" The one-word prayer stands for listening for
His voice, obeying what He says, relinquishing control, and
delighting in His will. Seeking His answer to every situation
and being willing to do things His way makes me walk my
path daily as He designed, all the while allowing Him to
refresh and renew my soul.

I must understand each person in every family will
experience some form of heartbreak. The more quickly I learn
that I don't have to walk my path alone, but can put my hand
into the hand of the One known in the scripture as the Good
Shepherd, the sooner my desperation turns to trust. The more
I learn to trust, the less shaken I'll be when another day of
testing comes along--when my husband has to go away, I find
a lump, or a someone needs stitches.

*Taste and see that the Lord is good; blessed is the
man who takes refuge in him. Fear the Lord, you his
saints, for those who fear him lack nothing. The lions
may grow weak and hungry, but those who seek the
Lord lack no good thing.* Psalm 34:8-10

The beauty of God's ways are that He gives individual
answers to each of His children for every problem. When I'm
the one with a problem, there's a temptation to form a
committee and get a consensus of how God wants to work.
Sometimes that's okay. Yet, often He calls me to come to
Him and quietly read His word and listen as He silently points

out the verses that apply to my situation. Sometimes He
allows me to draw from my well of previous lessons and
experiences, or uses the wisdom of others' spoken or written
words to speak to me. Occasionally, He quietly adjusts my
perspective, causing me to change my mind, eliminating my
struggle. As I taste of the Lord's goodness in solitude, the
times of sulking and wanting others to notice my misery grow
farther apart. I know God has the answer, and no matter how
He chooses to reveal it to me, I want it!

When stressful situations arise in other homes, nurturers
want to rush in and help. I'm a nurturer. I don't want to
neglect anyone who suffers or leave anything of importance
undone. I was always blessed when I was allowed to roll up
my sleeves and take action in the life of one of my military
sisters. My motives are usually pure, but even that's not
enough if it's not what God wants.

The flip side of my wanting to help and see the folks in
each of my communities be problem-free and one big, happy
family is that I tend to want to see instant fixes rather than
pray and wait patiently for the Lord's direction. In other
words, I get in the way. By waiting, however, I've learned He
does work thoroughly and on a perfect schedule.

Occasionally, I heard a distress signal sounding and thought
I was the only one who could answer the call. However,
running out to aid another, without prayer and subsequent
guidance from the Holy Spirit, led to frustration and
exhaustion. I learned through time, obedience, and
disobedience that if I listened to my Commander, He gave
simple, easy-to-follow instructions. If I weren't the one called
to go, but was faithful to pray, He answered mightily. Peace
came; the nagging thought that I couldn't "do it all" retreated.
I didn't have to know His plan or what He asked of others; I
merely had to obey what I thought He wanted me to do.

There were a few who demanded attention, having
expectations of me that I couldn't perform. They were often

disappointed. Even though I wanted each woman to taste and see that the Lord was good for herself, I had to learn that staying in God's will was more important than maintaining my reputation as a burden hearer.

I found that some folks are uncomfortable being alone with God yet hesitate to ask a friend for help. A sensitive burden bearer learns when to push in and when to back off. She watches to see if help is needed and if the one hurting is ready to receive encouragement. She understands that helping may be as simple as handing a tissue to dry tears or reading to children while their mom rests.

The fact remains that at some point each burden bearer with pure motives, a desire to help, and experience fails (even a mother). It's important that we know and pass on to our children and grandchildren that we'll do our very best to help, but it is only God Who never messes up. He alone is faithful to give the perfect measure of grace for us to walk each day in an imperfect world. What better gift can I give my kids and grandkids than the tasting of the knowledge and understanding that only our my Heavenly Father can lighten burdens? Only He solves my adult problems with the same gentle touch He did when I was a little girl--His way, not mine.

Finally, be strong in the Lord and in his mighty power. Put on the full armor of God so that you can take your stand against the devil's schemes. For our struggle is not against flesh and blood, but against the rulers, against the authorities, against the powers of this dark world and against the spiritual forces of evil in the heavenly realms. Therefore put on the full armor of God, so that when the day of evil comes, you may be able to stand your ground, and after you have done everything, to stand. Ephesians 6:10-13

*For though we live in the world, we do not wage war
as the world does. The weapons we fight with are not
the weapons of the world. On the contrary, they have
divine power to demolish strongholds. We demolish
arguments and every pretension that sets itself up
against the knowledge of God, and we take captive
every thought to make it obedient to Christ.*
II Corinthians 10:3-5

*Be self-controlled and alert. Your enemy the devil
prowls around like a roaring lion looking for
someone to devour. Resist him, standing firm in the
faith, because you know that your brothers
throughout the world are undergoing the same kind
of sufferings.* I Peter 5:8-9

God calls His followers to mirror His compassion; He also
directs them to stay alert and stand powerfully against the
devil! I could feel the warrior juices flowing. When I closed
the door on military life, I wouldn't lay down my weapon, the
Bible, or abandon training in prayer or let down my shield of
faith for I'd learned that life isn't a game, but a battle. The
enemy is constant. In God's army, there is never a change of
command or a need to rewrite my Commander's training
manual.

*Give thanks to the Lord, for he is good; his love
endures forever. . . . Let them give thanks to the Lord
for his unfailing love and his wonderful deeds for
men, for he satisfies the thirsty and fills the hungry
with good things.* Psalm 107:1; 8-9

My true freedom of choice, I learned, was the gradual process of learning to love and serve God, Mike, and the U.S.A. simultaneously. Since active duty began, we'd served in 12 locations and lived in 16 houses. My choice now would be to allow God to weave the old with the new. Yes, I needed to write down all those things stirring in my heart and vow to continue to hear the hearts of others.

Chapter 11

When I Grow Up

*The end of a matter is better than its beginning, and
patience is better than pride. . . Consider what God
has done.* . . Ecclesiastes 7:8; 13a

Fall, 1995: It is exhilarating to think Mike and I don't have
to move again if we don't want to. We travel without a
moving van nipping at our heels. The post I'd once merely
tolerated is just up the road, with its commissaries, exchanges,
and medical facilities. I'm encouraged each time I go to Fort
Hood to the ladies' meetings at the chapel for I find young
women there who love their husbands and our God.

Life, for me, two-and-a-half years into Mike's military
retirement, is a wonderful mixture of the old and the new. I no
longer watch men leave for work in battle dress uniforms (the
updated, unstarched work fatigues), but I have active duty
friends stationed at Fort Hood, and Mary Jane lives just up the
road. Even though Linda, Rita, and several of my other long-
time friends are scattered, the instant I hear one of their voices
on the telephone, even if it's been a year since we last talked,
it's as if our conversation stopped in mid-sentence, and we
pick it up again!

The number of wonderful neighbors and church family
around me keeps growing. Additionally, every other Saturday
some residents of our town meet to pray for our churches, our
community, our state, and our country.

It warms my heart to know that friends like Jim, Laura, and Carrie Henderson feel free to announce they're in town less than an hour before they pull into our driveway. Their squeezing a twenty-minute visit into their busy vacation schedule not only provided me a memory that I treasure but also affirmed the weaving of my yesterdays with my todays.

This past summer Mike took me to see Linda Seward in New York! We had a wonderful time catching up on family news. Ted's now a successful businessman; Michelle and Cathy teach school; I watched Annemarie get ready for her senior prom and be whisked away in a big limo; and we met Christelle, Michelle's daughter.

Grandma Vermillion hung up *her* prayer apron right before Christmas of 1993, only a few weeks after we'd moved into the new house. I was amused by her deathbed boldness. She tried to convince her oldest son, my daddy, to remarry. She knew he'd be much happier, and made one last effort to *mother* her child. But Daddy wasn't ready to take that big step. He and Genevieve waited until the spring of '94 to tie the knot, and I was pleased to be her matron-of-honor. Knowing that they are happy brings me great joy, and the fact that Genevieve and I are friends allows me the freedom and ease to make memories with her.

Thoughts of Grandma, Margaret, and Mother continue to warm my heart. Their possessions, mixed in with Mike's and mine in our new home, somehow bring comfort to this phase of our lives called retirement. They deposited a lifetime of love, values, and principles into our lives, and each could easily have been titled "the best grandma in the world." They set quite high standards for me to follow. Now, I understand their hearts. Although not an ideal situation, a grandma can be removed geographically from her grandchildren, and no distance is too great to separate her from the joy accorded her when her children have children. I've been granted the privilege of watching my grandchildren grow up without the stress of always being preoccupied with arranging our next visit.

Jordan (age nine) has taught me about baseball and soccer. One day soon he'd like to play football, but I can't get too excited waiting for that day to come. He and I have interesting conversations. The time I cherish most, other than the afternoon he was born, is the day he explained to me how he hears God's voice--it's down in his heart and others in the room can't hear it.

When he was five-and-a-half, Joseph told me that he was almost used to me; so we are friends at last. He, too, has a strong grasp of God's ways--he told Mario and Kathy the best thing about their church Easter play was when "Jesus was healed of His deadness." Smiling, vibrant Joseph, seven now and also an athlete, allowed me the honor of pulling his first loose tooth, and neither of us cried.

The boys' little sister, Sarah Elisabeth (*Elisabeth* for Mario's German Oma, who'd passed away), is truly a gift from God. Last spring she expressed her gratitude with *danka*, the German equivalent of "thank you." Now, with her brown curls bouncing, she talks as much as her mother, Kathy, did as a child. Although she denies it, Sarah's baby brother or sister will arrive soon, and she'll become the big sister.

Each of my children has expressed gratitude that his or her life was enriched by being an Army Brat. Kathy, wise beyond her years, still finds good-byes difficult. Mike continues to seek assurance Kristy forgave him for what she perceived to be his abandoning her at two years of age. Kristy's gentle compassion touches many.

The real test of my acquired flexibility and devotion to the United States military came mid-February, 1993. Just a few days before Sarah's birth and two weeks before Mike took off the Army's green, Rick donned a U.S. Navy uniform.

Weeks later, as Mike and I left Rick's graduation from Navy Boot Camp (the equivalent of Army Basic Training), I turned to my husband with an itty-bitty tear in my eye and announced I'd just changed my allegiance from the U.S. Army to the Navy. Mike feigned hurt. It may take me some time to learn Navy lingo, but I'll make it--I'm flexible!

In the heat of central Texas, wearing bifocals, sporting gray hair, and having driven many times across country in a car, sometimes all by myself, I am content.

Finally, I've learned what I want to be when I grow up--the best grandmother in the world!

Chapter 12

A Call to Action

I always thank my God as I remember you in my prayers, because I hear about your faith in the Lord Jesus and your love for all the saints. I pray that you may be active in sharing your faith, so that you will have a full understanding of every good thing we have in Christ. Philemon 4-6

My purpose is that they may be encouraged in heart and united in love, so that they may have the full riches of complete understanding, in order that they may know the mystery of God, namely, Christ, in whom are hidden all the treasures of wisdom and knowledge. I tell you this so that no one may deceive you by fine-sounding arguments. Colossians 2:2-4

More and more, I'm delighted when I see the courage with which young military wives/mothers accept the challenges and responsibilities that confront them. I applaud them as they serve their families and countrymen wherever Uncle Sam sends them. Many are women of faith.

Above all, love each other deeply, because love covers over a multitude of sins. Offer hospitality to one another without grumbling. Each one should use whatever gift he has received to serve others,

*faithfully administering God's grace in its various
forms.* I Peter 4:8-10

A few of the old military traditions have gone by the
wayside, but I don't think I've attended a single Fort Hood
Women of the Chapel meeting that I haven't heard a
testimony of God's greatness or a request to pray for one who
is hurting. It's common for a newcomer to attend, knowing
she will find others who will encourage her. Women of varied
ages and backgrounds gather there to share God's love with a
sense of urgency. They know that faces in the group come
from and go to other military communities routinely. They
pray, believing that God answers prayer, and study the Bible
confident they'll find dynamic, contemporary answers. They
love to talk about their mighty God instead of talking about
their overwhelming problems. They come to get filled with
encouragement so they can effectively serve their families and
community.

I'll be a better grandmother by hearing these young
women's hearts and allowing them to hear mine.

*And let us consider how we may spur one another on
toward love and good deeds.* Hebrews 10:24

*Let us therefore make every effort to do what leads
to peace and to mutual edification.* Romans 14:19

*Everyone who believes that Jesus is the Christ is
born of God, and everyone who loves the father
loves his child as well. This is how we know that we
love the children of God: by loving God and
carrying out his commands. This is love for God: to*

*obey his commands. And his commands are not
burdensome, for everyone born of God overcomes
the world. This is the victory that has overcome the
world, even our faith. Who is it that overcomes the
world? Only he who believes that Jesus is the Son of
God.* I John 5:1-5

*You see that his faith and his actions were working
together, and his faith was made complete by what
he did.* James 2:22

Those women of faith learn that following God's rules pays
rich dividends. They openly acknowledge that they need God
and each other, and generously offer practical help to one in
need. They train to speak the truth in love rather than loving
to speak the truth. They are women of action.

We've all had days when we suspected we were losing our
mind and our frustrations would never end. We've felt like the
Lone Ranger and couldn't imagine that praying "Lord?"
would restore sanity and put circumstances in perspective. It
sounds too simple. Yet, I must question: could some sanity be
restored to the workings of our government? Could disasters
both at home and abroad be avoided? Could the united-in-
prayer become an integral part of our nation's security? Could
our military be strengthened by women of faith doing more
than sending their men off to war with clean underwear and
being both mom and dad while they're away?

Would it demand "Wonder Woman"? Or, could it be that
women who faithfully pray merely need to focus on what God
wants, yearn to see Him move His mighty hand, and obey His
written commands and silent proddings?

Isn't it interesting to think about what would happen if
active duty and retired military wives, along with their mothers

and grandmothers, awakened asking the Lord what He wanted
them to do that day? Would we not see change in our homes,
on our military posts, in our civilian communities, and across
the entire nation? Couldn't we, no matter our age or length of
time associated with the military, move mountains (just like
He said in Matthew 21:21-22, with no doubting) by joining
forces?

Take a big breath. Come, hold my hand. Forward march.

*For it is time for judgement to begin with the family
of God.* I Peter 4:17a

In a country and world troubled mightily by the influences
of evil, sometimes our minds get distracted and we're tempted
to become discouraged. Without thinking, we assume there is
nothing we can do. We look around at all the immorality and
assess, "I'm not so bad." But as we look for God's divine
nature and His invisible, eternal power, our thoughts and
emotions get back into line with His. We measure our
attitudes, not by today's standards, but by the Words of God.

He tells us not to be overcome by evil, but to overcome
evil with good (Romans 12:21). Once we're scrubbed up, we'll
be eager to share the reality of His love with our new
neighbors.

*. . . If God is for us, who can be against us? He
who did not spare his own Son, but gave him up for
us all--how will he not also, along with him,
graciously give us all things? Who will bring any
charge against those whom God has chosen? It is
God who justifies.* Romans 8:31b-33

*For as high as the heavens are above the earth, so
great is his love for those who fear him; as far as
the east is from the west, so far has he removed our
transgressions from us. As a father has compassion
on his children, so the Lord has compassion on
those who fear him; for he knows how we are
formed, he remembers that we are dust.* Psalm
103:11-14

That's good news! I can almost see our fears running
away! Now that's something to write home about!

*. . . Jehoshaphat appointed men to sing to the Lord
and to praise him for the splendor of his holiness as
they went out at the head of the army, saying: "Give
thanks to the Lord for his love endures forever." As
they began to sing and praise, the Lord set ambushes
against the men of Ammon and Moab and Mount
Seir who were invading Judah, and they were
defeated.* II Chronicles 20:21-22

*"Not by might nor by power, but by my Spirit," says
the Lord Almighty.* Zechariah 4:6b

There are lessons to be learned from military training.
Members of the armed forces train until they learn to follow
orders instantly without question. They memorize the chain of
command and practice their own job skill until they can do it
efficiently and effectively. Battle plans vary to confuse the
enemy. Each unit has its duties and trusts the other to do its

job thoroughly and effectively. Good troops put in as much time as is needed to get each aspect of soldiering perfected.

Part of our prayer training is praising the Lord and being His cheering section. We don't have to be physical giants or to demand our human rights. We'll commit to prayer and not be thwarted when circumstances look intimidating. We'll learn to recognize and fight the real enemy. The devil wants to see military spouses defeated. He preys upon individual weaknesses when service members are away. Remembering he is the enemy, we must not expect trouble or disaster when the troops go to the field or the National Training Center, or when there is not enough money in the Defense budget for troops to train properly.

When we expect trouble, we play right into the devil's hands. Instead, we'll be strong, courageous, and expect God to send victory, each time in a different way to surprise us with peace, hope, and joy. That is His character, and He loves to answer the prayers of His children.

The foxhole is a place of both offense and defense, a place of safety with my invisible, powerful God calling the shots. He shares the plan of attack with me and tells me that only He has my eternal well-being at heart. In the quiet of my foxhole, I think about those plans and my part in the big picture. God whispers to me that I don't have to be afraid if I follow His leading. As a matter of fact, He tells me the ending not only of the battle, but of the war! He knows. He wrote the book and assures me that I'm on the winning team! Perhaps we'll need some scriptures to point to for direction. Foxhole meditation:

"Submit to God and be at peace with him; in this way prosperity will come to you. Accept instruction from his mouth and lay up his words in your heart."
Job 22:21-22

I have hidden your word in my heart that I might not sin against you. Psalm 119:11

The Lord is my light and my salvation--whom shall I fear? The Lord is the stronghold of my life--of whom shall I be afraid? When evil men advance against me to devour my flesh, when my enemies and my foes attack me, they will stumble and fall. Though an army besiege me, my heart will not fear; though war break out against me, even then will I be confident. One thing I ask of the Lord, this is what I seek: that I may dwell in the house of the Lord all the days of my life, to gaze upon the beauty of the Lord and to seek him in his temple. For in the day of trouble, he will keep me safe in his dwelling. . . Psalm 27:1-5a

So let us put aside the deeds of darkness and put on the armor of light. Romans 13:12b

Joshua said to them, "Do not be afraid; do not be discouraged. Be strong and courageous. . ."
Joshua 10:25a

...Who is this King of Glory? The Lord strong and mighty, the Lord mighty in battle. Lift up your heads, O you gates; life them up, you ancient doors, that the King of glory may come in. Psalm 24:8-9

O Lord my God, I called to you for help and you healed me. Psalm 30:2

Submit yourselves, then, to God. Resist the devil, and he will flee from you. James 4:7

The Lord delights in the way of the man whose steps he has made firm. Psalm 37:23

Sing to the Lord, you saints of his; praise his holy name. For his anger lasts only a moment, but his favor lasts a lifetime; weeping may remain for a night, but rejoicing comes in the morning. Psalm 30:4-5

Mighty, bold women who pray understand that people and circumstances are not the enemy; they know who is the true enemy, and as they pray, they put on Spiritual *armor* with a determination to see that enemy defeated in their communities.

Praying consistently makes it easier to keep the enemy out of our homes and posts, and the defense posture is fortified when praying folks watch for the devil's deceit. Perhaps the biggest lie he tells is that he doesn't exist! He prowls about pulling the same age-old tricks. Prayer and faith in what Christ provided on the cross prevent the devil, our enemy, from devouring us.

Resisting him and the evil thoughts he'd like to put into our minds requires constant attention. I can't resist evil thoughts if I don't recognize them as a plot of my enemy. Yet, our resisting makes room for the Holy Spirit to put in the good without hindrance. There is no struggle because the enemy has to flee.

When thoughts of a friend come to mind, we pray for her-- she's probably resisting the devil! When we're helped by answered prayer, we better understand how to pray for others.

We've been lonely and misunderstood; we've been isolated
from family; we've been unable to sleep when we were the
only one in the house; we've volunteered hundreds of hours
and sometimes saw no reward. But the beauty of our struggles
is that we know how to pray for military sisters--we know
their plight and picture in our minds what their needs might
be. Then we pray!

*You, my brothers, were called to be free. But do not
use your freedom to indulge the sinful nature;
rather, serve one another in love. The entire law is
summed up in a single command: "Love your
neighbor as yourself." . . . But the fruit of the Spirit
is love, joy, peace, patience, kindness, goodness,
faithfulness, gentleness and self-control. Against
such things there is no law. Those who belong to
Christ Jesus have crucified the sinful nature with its
passions and desires. . . . Since we live by the Spirit,
let us keep in step with the Spirit. Let us not become
conceited, provoking and envying each other.*
Galatians 5:13-14; 22-23; 25-26

*Everyone must submit himself to the governing
authorities, for there is no authority except that
which God has established. The authorities that exist
have been established by God. Consequently, he who
rebels against the authority is rebelling against what
God has instituted, and those who do so will bring
judgement on themselves. . . . This is also why you
pay taxes, for the authorities are God's servants,
who give their full time to governing. Give everyone
what you owe him: If you owe taxes, pay taxes; if*

revenue, then revenue; if respect, then respect; if honor, then honor. Romans 13:1-2; 6-7

"Because he loves me," says the Lord, "I will rescue him; I will protect him, for he acknowledges my name. He will call upon me, and I will answer him; I will be with him in trouble, I will deliver him and honor him." Psalms 91:14-15

The righteous man is rescued from trouble, and it comes on the wicked instead. Proverbs 11:8

"But whoever lives by the truth comes into the light, so that it may be seen plainly that what he has done has been done through God." John 3:21

Righteousness exalts a nation. Proverbs 14:34a

The king's heart is in the hand of the Lord; he directs it like a watercourse wherever he pleases. Proverbs 21:1

...Some trust in chariots and some in horses, but we trust in the name of the Lord our God. . . O Lord, save the king! Answer us when we call! Psalm 20:7;9

Open the gates that the righteous nation may enter, the nation that keeps faith. You will keep in perfect

peace him whose mind is steadfast, because he trusts
in you. Trust in the Lord forever, for the Lord, the
Lord, is the Rock eternal. Isaiah 26:2-4

Won't it be a surprise to those who trust in money and
politics when our nation is changed as a result of women's
prayers? With proper respect for authority and disdain for our
enemy's tricks, we will joyfully commit to the time required
for prayer. Stuffing the ballot boxes with prayer is not illegal
or expensive!

We'll pray fervently and expect those in authority to lead
us to repentance! If rulers are unjust, bringing instability to
our land, II Chronicles 7:14 promises if we'll do our part, then
He (God) will heal our land! Turning to eternal God and away
from the ways of the world, resisting the devil, praying, loving
and encouraging one another will bring yet unpublished
reports of His goodness and mercy. Personally, I can't wait to
hear what He does!

The seventy-two returned with joy and said, "Lord,
even the demons submit to us in your name." He
replied, "I saw Satan fall like lightning from heaven.
I have given you authority to trample on snakes and
scorpions and to overcome all the power of the
enemy; nothing will harm you. However, do not
rejoice that the spirits submit to you, but rejoice that
your names are written in heaven." Luke 10:17-20

Be exalted, O God, above the heavens; let your glory
be over all the earth. Psalm 57:11

Finally, brothers, whatever is true, whatever is
noble, whatever is right, whatever is pure, whatever
is lovely, whatever is admirable--if anything is
excellent or praiseworthy--think about such things.
Philippians 4:8

P.S. Aren't you excited about what God is going to do
when we seriously pray and believe He will answer? The same
God Who delivered the Israelites out of Egypt and Daniel out
of the lions' den continues to do great things all over our land!
I long to hear those reports rather than the doom and gloom I
hear from other places.

I am truly grateful to have had this opportunity to share my
heart with you. If you get down Georgetown, Texas, way, the
welcome mat is out! Just so you'll know, though, I may be a
little busy! Rick married September 30, 1995. His bride, Kim,
also serves our country in the Navy, and her five-year-old son,
Tyler, has already stolen my heart. Four days later Mario and
Kathy blessed our family with the birth of their daughter
Meagan Rose.

As the guys might say when ending a radio transmission,
"Over and out!"

Keep Praying!

About the Author

Helen Sayre Jackson was reared on a farm in central Indiana by loving Christian parents. She attended college for one year while her high-school sweetheart and future husband, Mike Jackson, was in the Carolinas as a Marine Corps reservist for six months. They were married in 1962. After the birth of two daughters, Kathy and Kristy, Mike joined the Army; five years later, their son Rick was born, completing their family.

During Mike's 25-year military career, Helen and the children accompanied him to eleven duty stations, and stayed home when Mike went to Vietnam. Helen served as a volunteer for the American Red Cross, Girls Scouts, and numerous chapels and churches.

Helen and Mike now live in Georgetown, Texas, near their daughters and grandchildren. They maintain contact with military friends all over the world. Helen's hobbies include cross-stitching, reading, and beginning golf. The book, *Army Green, Navy Blue*, in which she shares her faith and insights gained from her life as a military wife and mother, is her first.